M000200336

YOLO

Essential Life Hacks for Happiness

Vindy Teja, LL.B.

The
Unapologetic
Voice

EXPRESS YOUR VOICE WITH
INTEGRITY, TRUTH, CLARITY
Carrie Severson

Published in Arizona by The Unapologetic Voice House.

YOLO

Essential Life Hacks for Happiness

Vindy Teja, LL.B.

vindy@vindyteja.com
www.vindyteja.com

Editor: Tom Waldenfels

Book Cover Design: Kris Kovak

Author Photographer: Ronald Lee

Library and Archives Canada Cataloguing in Publication
ISBN 9781-9990985-0-6
e-ISBN 9781-9990985-1-3

Library of Congress Control Number:2019915106

If you would like to publish sections of this book,
please contact the publisher for permission.

Published by The Unapologetic Voice House
5101 N Casa Blanca, Scottsdale, AZ 85253

This book is dedicated to Kiran, my daughter,
who is a daily inspiration to be my true and best self...
to Karan, my father and unwavering supporter,
and to Raminder, my grandmother and best friend
throughout my formative years.

CONTENTS

FOREWORD

When Vindy told me she was writing a mindful living book, and in particular one called *YOLO: Essential Life Hacks for Happiness*, I was not at all surprised.

Vindy and I met almost three decades ago, when I was a Social Work student. She was in the 12th Grade and was selected by her mentors to co-lead a teen support group for her peers who were bridging Western and traditional cultures. We both shared a genuine belief in empowering others. It was apparent that Vindy was a natural leader, and I was drawn to her empathy and compassion, as well as her openness to hear one's story and affect change.

Over the years, I've seen Vindy's commitment to profound professional and personal growth through self-reflection, critical thinking, and challenging herself to master resiliency in the face of serious life setbacks. Vindy's book reflects who she is. Whether it's with her coaching clients, friends, or family members, she consistently demonstrates an ability to assess situations, help illuminate issues and empower others to create their own goals and develop clarity.

Vindy is intelligent and open-minded, with a well-rounded world view developed through life experience and her professional legal training. She is able to connect with diverse individuals in an unbiased manner coming from a place of curiosity and humility. Her resourcefulness, creativity, interpersonal skills and flexibility are characteristics she embodies and uses to help those in need. This uniquely positions her to share her knowledge and wisdom with you in this book.

Everyone seeks happiness. But how do you achieve it, sustain it and share it? So many life circumstances and obstacles can frustrate your desire and ability to be happy. We all experience setbacks from time to time, be it death of loved ones, illness, divorce, or financial loss. While it's true that some outcomes are beyond your control, this book will teach you that happiness is still something *you can do, and become*.

As a Social Worker, Educator and Facilitator, I have learned happiness comes from connecting with yourself and others. This leads to healthier communication and relationships overall, often starting with those closest to you. No matter what the situation, the common denominator is our basic desire to be happy. Vindy's book shares impactful information that will help its readers facilitate happiness. Her book teaches us that happiness is not about avoiding problems. It's about being intentional about your whole life...and what it has to offer.

She offers a practical and upbeat approach in *YOLO: Essential Life Hacks for Happiness*. She reveals the life hacks you want in your back pocket as you steer your way through life's complexities. Whether it's trying to get through the last semester at school, managing delicate relationships at home or work, or trying to silence the persistent inner critic, there's a hack you can use. I have no doubt you will find Vindy's book extremely useful in your everyday life as you develop your purpose and goals for happiness. Step into your vulnerability and enjoy this book.

Lucki Kang, RSW, MSW

Sessional Faculty Member
University of the Fraser Valley
University of Northern British Columbia

Co-Founder, CREATE Consultancy

ACKNOWLEDGEMENTS

How do you express your gratitude when you've finished writing your book, especially when you know many of the ideas and philosophies expressed might never have crystallized the way they did if it weren't for certain events taking place or certain people having the impact they did?

My late father, Karan, handed out chocolates to friends and family when I was born. This was at a time when the birth of daughters was not typically celebrated in my culture. He was an anomaly, and I was a beneficiary of that. I am grateful to you Dad for setting me on a path of lifelong learning and active living. Together with my mother, Inderjit, he immigrated from India to Canada to pursue a better life. I am forever grateful to them both.

"Bibbee," the name reserved for my late grandmother, Raminder, was my roommate and confidante throughout my youth. Thanks to her unconditional love, I had the freedom to play, learn and discover many of my passions. Special thanks to my anchors, Mom, Raj, Kiran and Arv. Thank you to all of my family and friends for their unwavering love, support and curiosity...and for being my sounding boards during tea time, walks, and just about anywhere I could corner you! I appreciate your patience.

Thank you Mr. Booth, my late mentor and high school teacher, for supporting me on my path to critical and independent thinking. Thank you Professors Constance Backhouse and Albert Oosterhoff for opening doors and gently nudging me through them. Thank you Madame Justice Eileen Gillese, former Dean at Western Law School, for being an unforgettable boss and mentor. You encouraged me to lean into my strengths, as well as maintain balance and purpose while pursuing my goals.

Thank you Jonathan Michael for your mentorship and for sharing your excitement and ideas when I proposed this project. Thank you Garrison Duke for your well-timed tips and words of encouragement.

In addition to the many people whose work or advice is cited, much appreciation goes to everyone who agreed to be interviewed as well as those who participated in my focus group. Your unique stories and insights are invaluable. Contributors include: Dr. Rupinder Toor; Lucki Kang; Peter Mwariga; Jonathan Michael; Mara St. Onge; Karima Bawa; Anna St. Onge; Suzanne Pelletier; Larry Beryar; Angie Chik; Sim Sandhu; Estrellita Gonzalez; Brinsley Stewart; Candace Plattor; Bill Inman; Farzana Logan; Kel Good; and Catherine Pulsifer.

Thank you to Saheli Circle and Chai & Chat, my amazing book clubs. You keep me thinking, discussing, and laughing. Thank you Neeti Jessa, Ronnie Sidhu, Ronald Lee Studios, and Ramzie Mach for making the photoshoot smooth and fun.

A special thanks to Tom Waldenfels, my editor, for his hand in this project. I especially appreciated your amusing and educational blue font commentaries. And to Kris Kozak for his book design, editorial input and technical support.

INTRODUCTION

There are lots of guidebooks out there about happiness, success and empowerment. Many convey similar messages, but with different audiences or perspectives in mind. So what makes this one special? I'm not an expert on your life and what will work for you. You get to fill those shoes. However, I am an expert on *mine*.
If I wrote a guide for my younger, motivated, yet naïve self...or the complete opposite, for my darkest days, when experiencing a multitude of negative and confusing states, this would be it.

Up until my thirties, I felt like I sailed through life. I was a cheerful kid. I excelled in sports, especially volleyball and track. School was fun and I did well, from Kindergarten right through to law school. I was valued by the law firm and universities I had worked for, and was blessed to enjoy solid relationships with family and friends. In first year university, I started dating "The Guy" ... and five years later I married him, the man I loved. My life certainly hadn't been absent of challenges, but I definitely considered myself a happy, mature and fulfilled person overall. So far so good, right?

It was after that period that I began to experience some serious challenges and setbacks. It began with the unexpected illness and death of my father. It was promptly followed with news that my husband and I wouldn't be able to conceive children without undergoing expensive fertility treatments. A few years later, I was blessed to give birth to my daughter, only to be followed by a divorce from hell a couple of years after that. A few years after surviving a grueling four-year divorce process, I was hit with a personal health scare that might leave my pre-teen daughter motherless. There's no way I signed up for this!

In the span of a decade and a half, I juggled a multitude of serious stressors that were virtually foreign to me. Loss, fear of the future, anxiety, anger, blame, confusion, uncertainty. At times, it was an overwhelming vortex of emotions. I was confused and wounded, but knew I didn't want to act or live from that place. I had to dig deep to find tools in my kit, and put them to immediate use. And I had to acquire some new ones if I had any hopes of emerging a stronger, happier and more peaceful person.

"Vindy, it's definitely time to write *that* book," I told myself. I needed clarity and solutions. I knew I wasn't alone, and that others around me faced similar challenges. These ups and downs were part of the universal human condition, or "full catastrophe living" as referred to by the founder of the modern mindfulness movement, Dr. Jon Kabot-Zinn. As a thoughtful and logical person, I concluded that if there was *any* chance my daughter would be unable to seek my input directly, I didn't want her consulting a Ouija Board to attempt to do so! The very least I could do is share my

"Whats", "Whys" and "Hows" about living life fully. The ones I considered to be the *most simple and powerful* – the essential life hacks to happiness.

Fortunately, my health issue got resolved. My passion for this project, however, remained undeniably strong. This book reflects what's worked well in my life, what's flopped and what's undergone fine-tuning. It represents my experience, observations, philosophies, studies and interviews. I'm a huge believer in collective learning and wisdom, so I've brought together other voices in this book. People who've experienced their own set of circumstances and challenges. They come from various cultural backgrounds as well as diverse professional backgrounds, such as education, law, business, medicine, government, entertainment, sports, coaching and social work.

Thank you for joining me on this journey.

Allow yourself to dream,
And when you do, dream big.

Allow yourself to learn,
And when you do, learn all that you can.

Allow yourself to laugh,
And when you do, share your laughter.

Allow yourself to set goals,
And when you do, reward yourself as you move forward.

Allow yourself to be determined,
And when you do, you will find you will succeed.

Allow yourself to believe in yourself,
And when you do, you will find self-confidence.

Allow yourself to lend a helping hand.
And when you do, a hand will help you.

Allow yourself relaxation,
And when you do, you will find new ideas.

Allow yourself love,
And when you do, you will find love in return.

Allow yourself to be happy,
And when you do, you will influence others around you.

Allow yourself to be positive,
And when you do, life will get easier.

-   Catherine Pulsifer
    Words of Wisdom, www.wow4u.com[1]

---

1 Reprinted with permission.

PART 1: HOME

SECTION A: LOVE

CHAPTER ONE

LOVE EACH OTHER

All you need is love
All you need is love
All you need is love, love
Love is all you need
- Beatles - *All You Need is Love*

Love is not a mere sentiment, but the ultimate truth at the heart of the universe.
- Rabindranath Tagore, Poet and Artist

1. *Love Love vs. Love*

"Love love versus love"? It's one of the best ways I can describe the difference in meaning of a word that gets thrown around all the time and loses its meaning. *"You'll* love *the new action movie playing downtown"* or *"Alex* loves *nachos with extra cheese"* is clearly not the same as "I love my mom and dad" or *"My sister* loves *her friend Sheryl. They've known each other since they were 9 years old."*

Maybe you *will* love the new action movie playing downtown. But right now, I'm concerned with "love, love" - the deeper emotion you feel for those close to you. It's incredibly powerful. It transforms lives, relationships and families. It energizes you.

There was once a middle-aged man named Lester Levenson. He was a successful entrepreneur but overall he found himself unhappy with his life. He had a number of serious physical problems. His doctors told him he didn't have long to live. He was "incurable." But Lester didn't want to die, so he asked himself this question ... What do I have to do to turn this around? What do I have to do to be healthy and happy again?

He decided he had to deal with all of his negative states and emotions, embracing them with unconditional love, and then releasing them. All the anger, the frustration, the fear, the defensiveness, the insecurity, you name it, it had to go, and in their place, nothing but love.

He lived into his 80s and went on to inspire hundreds of thousands with the release technique, helping them find their own way to inner peace, health, happiness and personal success by simply letting go of negative emotions and letting love fill the space left behind.[2*]

---

2 * https://www.sedona.com/Lesters-Story.asp.

he man was terminally ill, but something miraculous happened. Love made it all better. ove gave him new life and a new sense of purpose. And whenever you find yourself strug- ling, it can for you too. You don't have to struggle.

ove *is* the ultimate life hack. All you need is love. Love is all you need.

\s a child, Karima Bawa was forced to relocate to a new continent along with her family and many thers, starting a new life in Canada with very few financial resources. When reflecting on the most mportant and relevant lesson she took from this experience, she answered this way:

've concluded that the key lesson was understanding the importance of feeling secure. My family may not ave had much in terms of food, money or ability to do things, but what made it feel safe was the uncondition- l support and love my siblings and I always received. I never had the impression growing up that our lives nd circumstances were scary; instead, I got the impression it was an adventure. My parents never let on that e were at risk or that we were worth any less than people who had more. And it was these feelings I carried ith me into my core.

Karima's solid foundation served her well. She went on to become a successful lawyer, work hat took her all over the world. She is an engaged parent, active community member and hilanthropist. Having worked closely with her father in one of his businesses as a young voman, Karima always dreamed of starting her own business. After leaving the active practice f law, she did just that.

2. TWA Your Way into Love (Thoughts, Words, Action)

'm a big fan of the TWA 3-step process, a background program running in your life, so to peak. Thoughts – Words – Actions. Here's the jingle to go along with it: *the thought becomes he word which becomes the action.*

Though this program is running all the time, once you're consciously aware of it, it becomes a life hack that you can use way more effectively. With time and practice, you'll notice positive shifts, ones you can replicate in multiple areas of your life and with all the people in your world.

It's not a new concept. Here's the extend-a-mix version of TWA from Lau-Tzu, an ancient Chinese philosopher and writer.

Watch your thoughts; they become words
Watch your words; they become actions.
Watch your actions; they become habits.
Watch your habits; they become character.
Watch your character; it becomes your destiny.

You can use the TWA steps to your advantage in multiple venues: at home, school, work, out with friends or family, and even during your downtime when you're alone with your thoughts.

Chapter 1: Love Each Other

Life Hacks

Love is a deep emotion you feel, the power of which can be harnessed to transform lives, relationships and families. It energizes you.

Whenever you find yourself struggling, love can give you a new life and a new sense of purpose.

TWA your way into love (Thoughts, Words, Action). TWA is already taking place in your life but by becoming aware of it, you can use it more effectively and effortlessly in all areas of your life.

Your thoughts become words, your words become actions.

Questions and Exercises

1. Make a list of the most important relationships in your life. This especially includes the relationship with yourself! The list can be as short or as long as you like.

2. Identify the strongest or most loving relationships (or people) on that list.

3. What positive thoughts, words and actions do you associate with those relationships or people?

4. What aspects from those relationships can you apply to the ones that you want to improve?

Notes

Notes

CHAPTER TWO

THOUGHTS - THE BASELINE

As you think, so shall you become.
Bruce Lee - Actor, Martial Artist, Philosopher

Never let the things you want stop you from being grateful for what you have.
Unknown

Never underestimate the power of your thoughts. Your mind is the creator of your world. What you think determines your feelings and attitudes, which are expressed in your daily words and actions, multiplied by 365 days a year. Thinking of yourself or others as unworthy, incapable, unlovable, or unattractive leads to negative feelings. No surprise there.

Your feelings also help determine your thoughts. In that way it's like a loop. By paying attention to your feelings, rather than pushing them aside, you get precious data about what's going on in your internal world and what matters to you most...and that clarity can help direct your energy better.

Obsessing about goal-setting, achieving and the future robs you of enjoying the present. The end result: feeling sad, mad, bad, or a mix of all three! These emotions suck out your energy, energy you can no doubt spend on a million better things.

Cultivating kind, open and loving thoughts about yourself and others is not always easy, especially when you're tapped out, sick, had a disagreement with someone, or just had a stinky day in general.

But the proverbial magic wand *does* exist. Healthy techniques are available to you. Practicing them enables you to shift your perspective. Eventually, your experience allows you to go there effortlessly. I've included a few go-to techniques I use.

Whether you get a lousy mark on a school assignment or have a disagreement with your boyfriend, you'll know how to manage your disappointment, learn from the situation and process it with a constructive mindset.

The life hack here is surprisingly simple: *maintain an attitude of gratitude.* Or put another way, have a gratitude practice.

More times than not, gratitude is the answer to many self-destructive thoughts such as: complaining, criticizing, blaming, worrying, playing the victim and exaggerating differences between you and others.

1. *Gratitude Journal*

I'm sure you've heard of this life hack before, and there's a reason. It actually works!

Keeping a regular Grateful Journal, whether it's handwritten or on your device, is one of the most effective ways to positively transform your attitude. List a few different things every day or as often as you can. Let the list grow. Soon you'll be consciously seeking things to be grateful for, small and big. No paper and pen, or away from your device? Say them silently in your head, out loud, or share them with a friend. Though writing them down is more effective, something is better than nothing.

Gratitude is a big focus for Tony Robbins, a world famous motivational speaker, writer and coach. He offers the following prompts to help you consider what you're grateful for:

- Who do you love?
- Who loves you?
- What is the wealth you have currently in your life – technology? choices? friends? books? ideas? opportunities?
- What's right in your life?
- What's beautiful?
- What's magical?[3]

As a coach, I'm naturally curious about what others are grateful for. Mozhdah Jamalzadah, a professional Canadian Afghani singer and broadcaster, landed an Oprah-style talk show contract in Afghanistan. It enabled her to pursue one of her life-long dreams of making a difference in the everyday lives of Afghani women and girls. During her time there, she lived in Kabul, a city ravaged by conflict and war.

Upon returning to Canada, Mozhdah expressed her absolute appreciation for what we consider basic infrastructure, like reliable plumbing, internet access and drivable roads. She confessed that while doing laundry, she stared with admiration at the reliable water and heating pipes! Mozhdah's attitude of gratitude has helped her remain focused and keep disappointments in perspective. This has definitely allowed her to more easily navigate the ups and downs that come with working in the highly competitive entertainment industry.

2. *Gratitude Jar*

If journal writing isn't your thing, try using a Gratitude Jar. Have slips of paper and pen nearby. This is a great life hack for youngsters (or their parents, actually). Go crazy decorating the jar if you're an arts and crafts enthusiast. When you think of a gratitude, write it on a slip and throw it in. After a week or two, empty the jar and read them, share them with others if you like, feel really good, and then start all over again.

---

3 * http://sourcesofinsight.com/start-your-day-like-tony-robbins/

f you're looking for ideas and inspiration, check out the list of 1000 simple and underappreci-
ted things in the international bestseller *The Book of Awesome* by Neil Pasricha.[4]

3. *Opposition Game*

My friend, Sarah Lovely, an energetic and knowledgeable personal trainer, wellness business
owner and parent of three, introduced this game to me a few years ago. It's for all ages, played
solo in your head, or out loud with others. Every time a negative thought creeps into your
head, the kind that usually leads you down a toxic path of thinking for the next minute, hour,
day or week, become aware of it. Then, immediately challenge yourself to find a positive
thought to counter it. This is a quick and easy technique to switch your brain to gratitude
mode again.

The conscious brain is a curious thing. You can't hold two opposite thoughts *at the same time.*
For example, you can't simultaneously feel anger and patience toward someone who just cut in
front of you in the cashier's line at the grocery store. You switch from one to the other.

Here are a few examples to get you started.

Negative: You realize there are no grocery carts at the store entrance and you have to go back to
the parking lot in the pouring rain to get one.
Positive: At least you or your family can afford a full cart of groceries.

Negative: Two of your closest friends are late getting to your bowling birthday celebration,
delaying the start of the first game.
Positive: Given how busy work has been, you're excited and grateful to have a full afternoon of
fun with your friends.

In his book *The Monk Who Sold His Ferrari*[5], Robin Sharma describes this life hack as "Oppositional Thinking". The quality of your thinking determines the quality of your life. When
replacing a negative thought with a positive one, he encourages you feel what it's like in your
body and act differently. You might smile, move your body as if you're joyful, sit up straight,
or take in a few deep breaths. You get the idea.

---

4 [*] New York: Penguin Group (USA) Inc., 2010 1000awesomethings.com.
5 [*] Toronto: HarperCollins, 2007.

Chapter 2: Thoughts – The Baseline

Life Hacks

Maintaining an attitude of gratitude is a simple method to positively transform your attitude.

An attitude of gratitude can combat self-destructive thoughts you're having.

Use simple techniques to help you shift into gratitude, such as a gratitude journal, gratitude jar, or playing the oppositional game.

Questions and Exercises

1. Consider self-destructive thoughts you commonly find yourself having, such as complaining, criticizing, blaming, worrying, playing the victim, or exaggerating differences between you and others. Record them somewhere you can access them easily. Become self-aware when you're having them, and the impact they may be having on you.

2. Practice using one or more simple techniques below to shift into gratitude.

   a. *Gratitude Journal.* List a few different things you're grateful for in a journal or on your device, every day or as often as you can.

   b. *Gratitude Jar.* Record grateful thoughts you have on slips of paper, deposit into a jar, empty jar every week or two to review and share, repeat. Great for kids.

   c. *Opposition Game.* Played out loud or in your head, solo or multiple players. Every time a negative thought creeps into your head that threatens to lead you down a toxic or unproductive path of thinking, become aware of it and switch your brain to gratitude mode again by challenging yourself to find a specific positive thought to counter it.

Notes

Notes

CHAPTER THREE

THOUGHTS - THE NEXT LEVEL UP

A great many people think they are thinking when they are merely rearranging their prejudices.
-W William James

Once maintaining a basic attitude of gratitude becomes comfortable, and you start practicing it regularly, you're ready to take it up a notch with some additional life hacks.

1. *List of Victories*

Jonathan Michael, a professional coach, teacher and expert in a sophisticated personality test called The Birkman Method, often asks his clients to keep a List of Victories alongside their Grateful Journal. In it, they record all the work, school, family and personal things they've accomplished each day or week, no matter how small or big.

Finished a project two days early? Put it on the list.

Took time to help your partner sort, clean up and organize the mess in the garage? Put it on the list.

Stressed out, but took time to exercise or play your guitar and re-energize? Put it on the list.

Went through the mountain of emails in your Inbox? Put it on the list!

Most of us downplay or forget our accomplishments, major and minor, because our lives are busy and our "To Do" list seems unending. There's always more to do and what we've accomplished never seems to be enough. The result? Frustration and dissatisfaction. On days you're feeling down, refer to the List of Victories. This helps combat self-doubt or the feeling that nobody believes in you. What's more, your list gently produces more compassion, patience and love, for yourself and others. After all, if you can't feel these things for yourself, how can you possibly expect to offer them to your family and loved ones?

2. *Don't Take Anything Personally*

"If you live for the applause, then you'll die by the silence."
- Unknown

"What people think of me is none of my business."
- Attributed to Hellen Keller and Wayne Dyer

Keep this acronym in your back pocket: Q-TIP. **Q**uit **T**aking **I**t **P**ersonally.

If you can practice this "tip" regularly, you're on your way to becoming a pretty peaceful human being. When people say or do things that hurt your feelings or interfere with your life, you may assume it's because of something you are or did or said. But what if what they say and do is just a reflection of their own reality, based on things like their past experiences, upbringing, values and beliefs, and so forth? Often they may or may not even be aware they're doing this.

In his long time bestselling book, *The Four Agreements*[6], Don Miguel Ruiz elaborates on the agreements we can make with ourselves to enjoy a better quality of life. Among them is the principle of not taking things personally. Ruiz explains that it's not always easy to figure people out. A lot of the time, even *they* don't know what motivates them. So why waste your precious energy on such exhausting guesswork? Rejecting this guesswork pays off. You avoid attaching your self-worth to how others view you.

I've summarized the four agreements. Ruiz elaborates on all these self-limiting beliefs in his book, and I recommend it to readers who want to delve deeper.

The Four Agreements are as follows:

1. **Be Impeccable with your Word** (speak with integrity).

2. **Don't Take Anything Personally** (nothing others do is because of you).

3. **Don't Make Assumptions** (search for the courage to ask questions and to express what you really want).

4. **Always Do Your Best** (do your best in the circumstances).

Ridding yourself of the messages you've received from others that are genuinely not true for you is a HUGE benefit of practicing the Q-TIP life hack. Over time, you naturally feel stronger connections with some people than others. You also end up respecting the advice and opinions of those *you* respect. The others? Well, maybe you can just learn to silently smile at their perception of you.

The moral of the story? Spend energy on becoming more self-aware and exercising self-management, rather than taking things personally. Then you can use more of your brain power to tune into others and effectively manage your relationships with them.

Suppose you're on a basketball team and the coach unexpectedly substitutes you out. You could try to tap into *why* you might be feeling threatened or upset when that happens, rather than assuming

---

6 * Amber-Allen: 1997, San Rafael.

he coach doesn't value your efforts or "has it out for you." Allowing your mood to dictate your behavior often backfires. You go into "attack mode" rather than "understand mode".

Don't get me wrong. It's important to stand up, communicate your needs and have your boundaries respected. That's Empowerment 101. But rather than taking things personally, try facing the situation head-on. Asking questions, reflecting and seeking clarification from your coach will usually get you further. Not to mention that it may strengthen relationships with your teammates and coach.

Let me illustrate with one more example that probably sounds painfully familiar to younger readers, or adults whose parents still treat them like they're 12!

Your mom has repeatedly asked you to finish your homework. You're irritated. You have a choice about the meaning you put on her request:

- She assumes I won't finish it without being told. She thinks I'm irresponsible.
- She's trying to boss me around. She thinks I'm immature.
- She never says this to my brother. She favors him.

What if mom just wants you to finish, so the whole family enjoys the homemade pizza she's made? Or she has an important meeting later and needs to get out the door soon. Or fill in with any number of scenarios you've encountered.

Taking things personally might make you feel misunderstood, unappreciated, frustrated, impatient or sad. But, instead, why not try telling your mom what you're noticing in her tone of voice and repeated demands? Politely ask her what's up. This takes the focus off you. Your thoughts and attitudes may soften and you lose that Win/Lose stance. You opt for trying to find mutual understanding in place of conflict.

3. *Think Win-Win or No Deal*

As you've seen so far, your thoughts and resulting attitudes impact your outcomes. This applies to daily interactions and long term relationships. Family relationships are usually long term. Adopting a Win-Lose attitude here may get you short term gains, but result in longer term damage to these relationships.

For example, using your status as youngest sibling to get family rule exceptions may win you perks and keep you out of major trouble in your youth. Over time, however, you risk losing sibling loyalty and credibility points from your parents. They come to view you as "the baby" (even when you're 31 or 41), unable to take responsibility or make independent decisions. This learned helplessness can creep into other areas of your life and diminish your confidence and ability to take on challenges.

Win-Lose is competitive by definition, where someone is "the victor" and the other "the loser." How do you enjoy being the loser? Exactly.

In *The 7 Habits of Highly Effective Teens*[7], Sean Covey applies the classic principles his father Stephen Covey originally introduced in *The 7 Habits of Highly Effective People*[8]. He does this in a way that appeals to adults and teens alike. Sean Covey envisions Win-Win as "the all you can eat buffet", in which you're confident enough to adopt a belief that everyone can win, and there's enough cake to go around for everyone. With this approach, you're actually motivated to find solutions that work for all involved, not just you. That means you're more likely to collaborate. When you want others to reach their goals, it ends up making you feel good in the process. In any long-term or important relationship, a Win-Win attitude usually leads to stronger, healthier and closer relationships over a lifetime.

"No Deal" refers to a situation in which the people agree beforehand that they simply walk away if a mutually beneficial solution can't be found. A common disagreement is how to spend group time with your friends or family. For example, Sis wants to watch a vampire TV show, Bro wants to watch an action comedy, Dad wants to go bowling, and Mom wants you all to take turns giving her a shoulder massage! If you cannot all agree, you pre-agree you'll go out for a specific movie together. That's No Deal. Not so bad, huh?

A Note on Problem Solving

Problem solving is one of those skills you can never have enough of! Overcoming obstacles, working through an issue with a friend or co-worker, managing group member expectations – all of these require effective problem solving skills. Karima Bawa shares her process:

When dealing with an issue I need to work through with someone else, I figure out what their objectives are, understand the points most critical to me, and then try to come up with a solution that meets their top objectives and allows me to get as much of what's important to me. Listening closely and understanding the other person's perspective will almost always help me reach a more mutually acceptable solution.

When dealing with an important and long term relationship, I always keep in mind that the issue I'm trying to solve will be only one of many in the history of my relationship. Building goodwill is key. Doing the right thing, not taking shortcuts, not taking advantage – these are all things that people usually remember I've done and often come back to me in a positive way at a later time from that very person. Not always, but much of the time.

When dealing with the type of problem that doesn't require having a dialogue with another person or people, I usually allow the issue to "process in the background." I can think about it, even a lot, over a period of time, when I'm doing other things. I take notes when ideas come to me, and they often come at the strangest times. Eventually, I usually narrow it down to 3 or 4 points. I have learned to trust my gut and intuition.

Larry Beryar, a fraud investigator and manager, parent and former competitive hockey goalie, echoes Karima's Win-Win philosophy and applies it to the competitive sports context. *"It's not about winning at all costs, it's also about how you play the game. There is a humanness at the end of it."* As a player, Larry found he cared about his teammates and the camaraderie he shared with them,

---

7 [*] Fireside: New York, 1998.

8 [*] Free Press: New York, 1989, 2004.

but he didn't have an appreciation for the dynamics of the relationships for all the groups involved. Years later, as a coach to his son's hockey teams, he found himself managing the kids, their various skills and motivation levels and parent expectations, not to mention the relationships among kids, parents, referees, administration and opposing teams. Win-Win thinking definitely proved to be useful!

Chapter 3: Thoughts – The Next Level Up

Life Hacks

A List of Victories helps you combat self-doubt and become your own advocate, particularly when you're feeling down, unproductive, or unmotivated.

Q-TIP (Quit Taking It Personally). When people say or do things that have hurt your feelings or interfere with your life, it is a reflection of their own reality.

Think Win-Win or No Deal. Adopting a Win-Lose attitude may get you short-term gains, but result in longer term damage to relationships. Win-Win motivates you to find solutions that work for all involved, not just you. No Deal is when people agree beforehand on what happens if a mutually beneficial solution cannot be found.

Questions and Exercises

1. Note down items you accomplish each day or week, no matter how big or small. Name it a List of Victories journal (could just be the back of your Gratitude Journal). Refer to it whenever you need a boost.

2. Think of a situation or disagreement that you may have misunderstood or lacked all the details. What are the values and beliefs, past experiences, or upbringing that might account for the reactions?

3. Pinpoint a time when you collaborated well with others. What strategies did you or the others use to come up with solutions? How did you deal with any reluctance? What was the end result? Compare that with a time when you adopted a Win-Lose or All or Nothing attitude instead.

Notes

Notes

CHAPTER FOUR

WORDS

"Words are but pictures of our thoughts."
- John Dryden

What, how and when you say something can make all the difference in a conversation. You know what it feels like to be misunderstood, ignored, talked down to, talked over, or talked at. Not good. The tone and volume in which you're spoken to further impacts how you process messages you receive.

Peter Mwariga, a business owner and developer, coach and parent, describes how he learned the power of words at a young age:

I was the 5th child out of 6th in a very rambunctious house, so I learned to listen and negotiate a lot, rather than reacting and swimming upstream, because I knew it was a battle I always lost growing up. I learned early that if human beings go into defensive mode, they will fight whatever you're saying or trying to do. A person has to feel like they are a part of what you want to do. You have to cultivate that connection. Even your mannerisms before you speak will affect how a person reacts to you.

Both in business and personal relationships, I realized that to be successful, you have to "have a like" for the person you're dealing with. A lot of us come into situations being closed off and with intent, which may help you do your job, but it won't be effective at opening people up. People see your intent. They think 'he wants something from me, and I don't like that.' It's important to take the time to give a person that 'warm and fuzzy feeling' first. Have a genuine curiosity about people and life. These are the most successful people, professionally and personally. They have the curiosity of a child, which is magical.

1. *Pick your words wisely*

"People may hear your words, but they feel your attitude."
- John C. Maxwell

With simple word choice, your statement can go from sounding judgmental or argumentative to one that sounds conversational or solution directed.

Nan Einarson, a professional coach and educator, guides her clients and students on the power of word usage to contain judgement. She uses a life hack - or simple formula -you can start practicing right away.

Substitute "Should" with "Could"

"Should" sounds more aggressive and when you use it, you put people on the defensive and imply you know more than they do, whereas "could" suggests possibility, hope and curiosity.

"What should you have done?" sounds more judgmental than *"What could you have done?"*

Substitute "But" with "And"

"But" discounts and devalues everything you say before it, whereas "and" honors a person's opinion or qualities, communicates acknowledgement and provides additional perspective.

Consider which statement lands better:

"I appreciate your input, but we have to consider other people's viewpoints."
OR
"I appreciate your input, and we have to consider other people's viewpoints."

Substitute "Why" with "What"

"Why", especially when accompanied with a judging or blaming tone of voice, implies you made a mistake and prompts you to defend your position. "What" sets up an open-ended question and implies curiosity.

"Why are you saying that?" (especially when coupled with a raised voice) declares war versus *"What do you mean by that?"* which sounds more inquiring than demanding.

Substitute "You with "I"

Hearing "you" often gets your back up and you fall into defensive mode. "I" speaks to what you observe, think, feel and want.

"You did not pick up the equipment in time for the presentation." Vs *"I did not get the equipment in time for the game."* Subtle alterations can really make a difference in how your message is received and responded to.

Experiment and incorporate the non-judgmental words into your conversations. You'll notice a gradual shift in your attitude towards others. *and* the responses you get back.

I wrote the words above on Post-It Notes and stuck them around the house for a few months. By calling me out on my "shoulds", "whys" and "buts", my daughter became more conscious of her word choices, too. Given our competitive natures, we both sought to use the offending words as little as possible. The payoff was worth it. We developed a stronger habit of using kinder words.

2. THINK Before You Speak

Girl Talk[9]*, an international non-profit peer-to-peer mentoring program, had a great national campaign called T.H.I.N.K.. Your challenge is to ask yourself the following before you speak, text or write something:

T – is it true?

H – is it helpful?

I – is it inspiring?

N – is it necessary?

K – is it kind?

Words are *extremely* powerful. Becoming more conscious of this power prepares you to use it more responsibly. I like to keep this life hack in my back pocket for times when I'm about to blurt out some potentially damaging words.

3. You have two ears and one mouth for a reason.

I'm sure you've heard this sarcastic statement before. But it's actually a highly effective life hack. It simply means you might want to listen more than you speak. The Dalai Lama, a world renowned thinker and Buddhist spiritual leader, puts a kinder twist on it: *"When you talk, you are only repeating what you already know. But if you listen, you may learn something new."*

Become a Good Listener

Becoming a good listener is HARD. It requires patience, discipline and A LOT of practice. Many people never get good at it, nor do they seem to try. Listening conveys respect. In close relationships, the gift of listening is an act of love. It means you listen with a commitment to hearing exactly what the other person is saying.

Challenge yourself to gradually become self-aware of habits that interfere with good listening. Try to catch yourself if you're doing the following:

- Interrupting
- Finishing the other person's thoughts
- Multitasking
- Having an internal dialogue, the whole time (*"I'm hungry." "Why didn't I think of that?" "Wow, that happened to me too."*).

---

9 * www.mygirltalk.org.

Becoming an expert listener is a fantastic skill. Here are some pointers to hone your skills further:

Step 1: Hear what a person says.

Step 2: Focus on both what a person says AND what he or she does or doesn't say.

Step 3: Listen deeper for clues about the other person's thoughts, concerns and assumptions, which may have led to the conversation in the first place. This also helps you ask clarifying questions, another sign you're genuinely listening and trying to understand.

Step 4: Aim to genuinely give the other person the experience of truly being heard and understood.

Remember, active listening doesn't mean you agree with everything the other person says. It just means you're listening attentively and practicing empathy.

Ask questions. A lot of them.

The art and science of asking questions is the source of all knowledge.
- Thomas Berger

One of my daughter's passions is public speaking. In the 6th Grade, she chose me as her topic. I was surprised, honored and a tad worried too. She spoke about lessons she'd learned, including the significance of love and communication as keys to building good relationships with parents. This especially held true during the tween and teen years when there seems to be a lot of "intense disagreements," as she put it. When they're *least* likely to feel warm and fuzzy towards their parents, she advised her fellow students *that* was the perfect time to try to *communicate, ask questions and be loving.* It was a proud sappy mom moment for sure!

Peter Mwariga describes "being schooled" at school. Peter survived the rough and often unforgiving culture of an all-boys, ethnically diverse boarding school in Kenya, Africa from the ages of 12-16. He describes the challenges he faced and lessons he left with:

This was a very difficult and pivotal time for me, and I didn't really progress until I found my place within the organization, so to speak. I went to the same school as all my siblings, where they excelled athletically and academically. There was pressure from home and at school to do just as well as they did. It was relentless. I was dyslexic, and it was undiagnosed and not understood much then, so many assumptions were made about my ability to academically succeed. It took a long time for me to find my place and be comfortable being "me." Life challenges you that way continually. Because I developed this thick skin from a young age, I realized I've managed to exist comfortably within myself.

Part of what this experience enabled me to do is distinguish myself and hone my negotiation, mediation, and comedic skills. If there was one thing I knew, it was that I could always get people to laugh, no matter how tense the situation. In the course of my life, I've found that people are the easiest and most comfortable thing for me to deal with, which is surprising, because a lot of people aren't comfortable with others, especially those who are quite different from them. I've found I not only connect easily, but intensely, in a matter of minutes. The key for me has always been to be curious, open and ask a lot of questions.

Not only does asking questions foster good communication, it prevents you from making too many assumptions and drawing false conclusions. The answers you receive lead to clarification, new information, increased understanding and potential solutions. Though all this deeper inquiry seems like more work, the benefits far outweigh the disadvantages.

Powerful questions are open-ended, simple and direct. Avoid close-ended questions. They lead to "yes" or "no" answers, may sound accusatory and may even end conversations instead of moving them forward. Here are some examples of close-ended questions:

Are you going to do something about it?

Is there a better way to go about this?

You know I asked you not to do that, right?

Do you have any questions?

Are you telling me you thought this was a good idea?

Open ended questions often start with "What is", "When", "How", or "Where". They invite the person to clarify what they meant, reflect on what they're saying and its impact and exercise more empathy towards you and others. Examples include the following:

What would happen if I were to do this?

When something like this happens, how do you usually react?

What questions do you have?

How would you feel if the tables were turned and somebody said that to you?

Or you can make a request. It's like asking a question.

Tell me about a time you've felt like this before.

Tap into your inner investigator and practice asking open-ended questions, especially during "intense disagreements," as my daughter puts it!

Strangulation by Triangulation

Don't worry, this is not the part where you're subjected to a random geometry lesson. "Triangulation" is also a psychology term to describe the situation *"where an outside person intervenes or is drawn into a conflicted or stressful relationship in an attempt to ease tension and facilitate communication.*[10]*"* Although there can be many positive outcomes from seeking help or involvement from a third party, especially one who is genuinely caring and insightful, there's also a dark side to consider.

Triangulation can refer to a manipulation tactic where one person will not communicate directly with another person, and uses a third party instead to convey communication to the second person, thereby forming a triangle.

Finally, triangulation also refers to a situation when you play one person against another, prompting rivalries or tension between people. Consult any Shakespeare play or TV drama series to see an abundance of triangulation. Unfortunately, it happens all too often in everyday life and relationships, too.

What does triangulation have to do with love and communication? It stops – or strangulates - the flow of both. It causes untold harm personally, in relationships and in organizations such as families, schools and workplaces.

For example, when we talk about people when they're not present, we don't give them the opportunity to respond to what we're saying. This is how gossip starts and spreads. We make unfair assumptions. We hurt feelings. Relationships become strained. The people affected get stressed and anxious. The list goes on.

Awareness is the first phase of stopping strangulation by triangulation. Whether you see this behavior in yourself or others, whether it's a small or big, the next phase is clear. Make a conscious effort to *get out of the way*, or ask the interfering party to do so.

Psychotherapist Susan Forward writes about this topic in her book, *Emotional Blackmail*[11]. She provides strategies to deal with triangulation. Refuse to carry messages back and forth. Decline the "opportunity" to become the problem solver. Take some space to think, process your feelings and prioritize. For example, you can excuse yourself to get a drink of water or go to the bathroom.

When the third person gets out of the way, what happens to the triangle? Exactly, it becomes a line. A line of direct communication and accountability.

---

10 * Good Therapy: August 1, 2016, http://www.goodtherapy.org/blog/psychpedia/triangulation.
11 * HarperCollins: New York, 1998.

Chapter 4: Words

Life Hacks

Pick your words wisely. With simple word choice, a statement goes from sounding judgmental or argumentative to one that sounds conversational or solution directed.

THINK before you speak. T – is it true? H – is it helpful? I – is it inspiring? N – is it necessary? K – is it kind?

Become a good listener. Listen without interrupting, finishing the other person's thoughts, multitasking and having an internal dialogue in your head the whole time.

Ask questions. A lot of them. Powerful questions are open-ended, simple and direct. Avoid closed questions which lead to a yes or no answer, may sound accusatory, or end conversations instead of moving them forward.

Strangulation by triangulation. Avoid intervening or being drawn into a conflicted or stressful relationship to ease the tension or facilitate communication. Encourage a line of direct communication and accountability instead.

Questions and Exercises

1. In your everyday conversations, try substituting "should" with "could", "but" with "and", "why" with "what", "you" with "I". Observe subtle and not-so-subtle shifts that occur.

2. What do you do during conversations? Do you listen without interrupting? Finish the other person's thought? Multitask? Have an internal dialogue in your head the whole time?

   Do you do this with particular people? How do you feel when you sense others doing this with you? If you catch yourself doing these things, practice bringing yourself back to the present conversation, until it becomes a habit.

3. Think of someone who often uses powerful questions. It could be you. Questions that start with "What is", "When", "How", "Tell me about", or "Where". Notice the words they use, their tone of voice, their body language, their patience level, and the follow up questions they ask.

4. Identify situations or relationships in which you've been drawn into a conflict or stressful relationship, only to find yourself feeling manipulated, blamed, or unexpectedly caught in the middle. What if you refused to carry messages back and forth? Or declined the opportunity to become the problem solver? Or simply took some time to think and process your feelings? How might the outcome have been affected?

Notes

Notes

CHAPTER FIVE

ACTIONS

Show me, don't tell me.
- Unknown

Actions speak louder than words. Just because someone says something doesn't make it so.

Your words alone may sound good. Amazing actually. They may inspire and persuade, but nothing speaks louder than practicing what you preach. That's how you make a difference in the world. You lead by example. The opposite also holds true. A pattern of *incongruence* or lack of harmony between your words and actions gives others the impression you're dishonest and hypocritical.

1. *Talk the Talk, Walk the Walk.*

Talk the talk and *walk the walk* means the way you conduct yourself agrees with what you're saying. It's a work in progress. Some of the work is easier, other parts are deeper and require ongoing commitment and practice. The payoffs of this life hack are huge. Here are some helpful tips mixed in with some food for thought:

- It's a question of integrity. Integrity means consistently choosing your thoughts and actions based on values rather than personal gain. Personal gain may be the result, but that's not your main motivator.

- Make a promise only if you intend to keep it. Once you've made it, keep it! If circumstances change and you're unable to, communicate directly with the person you made the promise to. Explain what's changed. This is a big part of being in integrity.

- Criticizing the words and actions of loved ones when you yourself use the same language and behave similarly is hypocritical. Do your best and lead by example.

- Be curious. Try to figure out what's led someone to do or say something. Are they feeling threatened? Disrespected? Exhausted? Sad? To get back on track, maybe they just need a reassuring word, hug or nap!

- You can't expect to behave yourself into bad situations and talk your way out of them. If you borrow your dad's car and consistently bring it back late, be prepared to have your privileges revoked for a while. And you'll probably have to ask for the opportunity to earn his confidence again.

Karima Bawa offers a favorite expression from a friend about this subject: *"Be able to look yourself in the mirror. Never feel you have to look at the rear view mirror to see what's coming at you."* Doing something you know you may regret later, that go against your core values[12]*, is never a good idea. Though it seems difficult to resist those tempting shortcuts, doing so is definitely worth it. You save yourself a lot of lost sleep and fear about the future.

2. *Recipe for Your Best Self*

The ingredients, or qualities, that go into making your best self naturally varies from those that apply to your friends, partner, or co-workers. When I was training with CDC Certified Divorce Coach®, the instructor had us do a Best Self Exercise. It was intended to increase our self-awareness and self-management skills, as well as our ability to coach our peers and future clients.

I've included an adaptation of it (with permission) because it's a great life hack. Take a few minutes to complete it, use it as your reference point, and consider sharing it with those helping you achieve your best and vice versa. Note that different expressions of "best self" can be used. Some people use "true self" or "highest self." Use the terms that resonate with you.

1. Think of a few people (3-5) who have had a positive impact on you and jot their names down. For each one, identify 2-3 qualities you admire about them. We tend to notice in others the attributes we also consider important: *If you can spot it, you got it.*

2. Write down the qualities your family and friends are seeing in you when you're being your best self, as well as those you see in yourself. This is who you are when you're on your "A" game, feeling good and walking your talk. Be as specific if possible. Examples might include the following:

    i. Thoughtful (kind words, lending a helping hand)
    ii. Enthusiastic (cheer others on, proactive)
    iii. Funny (crack jokes, use wit to ease stress)
    iv. Dependable (show up, consistent, keep promises)
    v. Focused (use time wisely, pay attention, ask questions)

3. Consider the kinds of negative behaviors you exhibit when you're not being your best self. These are red flags to be aware of and to work on over time. Here are some suggestions from the CDC Certified Divorce Coach exercise:

    a. Justification of myself. Common justifications include:
        i. I am better than that/I am better than you
        ii. I am less than others
        iii. I deserve more than what I am getting
        iv. I have to do it all
        v. I must be seen a certain way

---

12 * For a helpful exercise on identifying, grouping, and narrowing down your values, see https://www.cmu.edu/career/documents/my-career-path-activities/values-exercise.pdf

b. Blaming others
c. Criticizing
d. "Horriblizing" or Catastrophizing
e. Being right – making the other wrong
f. Being a victim
g. Exaggerating differences

Working on these things might include becoming aware of what's missing for you. It might be rest or sleep, physical activity, time alone, or social connection. Or maybe you need to manage the things that are stressing you out, like school projects, family obligations, work deadlines and health concerns.

When you deny or ignore issues, you're not working on them. Instead, you're inviting them to show up in other behaviors and relationships. This is another work-in-progress and perfection is *not* the goal. A little compassion for yourself goes a long way.

3. Keep Calm and Practice Self-Care.

The main prerequisite course to loving others well is loving *ourselves* well. Sounds kind of weird, doesn't it? I'm not pushing you to be selfish, self-centered, or self-absorbed. I'm talking about practicing *self-preservation* through *self-care*. This is essential to your wellness, which includes staying healthy, regulating your mood and coping effectively with the effects of everyday stress. If you're not treating yourself well on the inside, it makes sense you won't be healthy or happy on the outside. You also won't be much help to others.

Candace Plattor is a therapist specializing in addictive behaviors, fellow TEDx speaker and author of the award-winning book *Loving an Addict, Loving Yourself: The Top 10 Survival Tips for Loving Someone with an Addiction*[13]. In her book, she points out the announcement we hear before an airline flight, advising us to always secure our own oxygen mask before assisting others.

I see this as a perfect analogy of healthy self-care. It simply makes sense: if you cannot breathe yourself, how are you going to be able to help anyone else continue to breathe? In this case, it is not selfish to put yourself ahead of others. You must take care of your own needs first; only from there will you be capable of giving yourself to others who need your help[14].

Self-care refers to the practice of caring for your body, brain, heart and soul. The next chapter provides an overview of these areas and includes information and tips you can use right away.

---

13 * Candace Plattor: 2015, Vancouver.
14 * 125-126

Chapter 5: Actions

Life Hacks

Talk the talk, walk the walk. The way you conduct yourself matches what you're saying.

Increase your self-awareness and self-management skills to become your Best Self.

Keep calm and practice self-care. Practicing self-preservation through self-care means taking care of your body, brain, heart and soul.

Questions and Exercises

1. Come up with three examples of when you followed through on the promises you made? How did it feel? What were the payoffs? Think of times when you didn't. How did it impact the other person or the relationship? How could you have done things differently?

2. Recipe for Your Best Self

    a. Think of a few people who have had a positive impact on you

    b. Identify 2-3 qualities you admire about each of them.

    c. Write down the qualities your family and friends are seeing in you when you're being your best self. Be specific.

    d. Consider the negative behaviors you exhibit when you're not being your best self which you can work on.

3. Which self-care habits currently work well for you?

Notes

Notes

CHAPTER SIX

ACTIONS - PRACTICING SELF-CARE

The most common way people give up their power is by thinking they don't have any.
- Alice Walker

Practicing self-care is a huge and fundamental topic. There are so many resources out there dedicated to each and every heading in this chapter. New research and discoveries add to our knowledge every day. Sometimes there seems to be so much information and so many conflicting viewpoints, you haven't a clue where to start. During those times, it helps to keep the acronym KISS in mind: **K**eep **I**t **S**imple **S**illy.

Self-care is not a one time or some time thing. It's something you do on an ongoing basis. Once you review the basics here, consider your own self-care regime. And the power you have over it. Add or tweak things, integrating more practices over time. When your needs, health and priorities change, adjust accordingly. The phrase, "you are what you eat, feel, think and do," gradually starts to make sense when you take this section and integrate it with the others in this book. Remember: Quitting won't speed things up.

Physical, intellectual, emotional and spiritual strength are key to your success in *life*. Reread that last sentence. Defining "success" broadly this way is an advantage. Your priorities will naturally shift over time, based on your age, life stage, knowledge and experience. However, striving for a healthy balance within that space will always serve you well.

Although this book covers goal setting, action plans and cultivating your strengths, it also emphasizes the other essentials of success: fostering clear and healthy communication, building strong relationships, playing and seeking adventure, giving back, taking care of yourself and so on. Throughout, you'll detect a reoccurring theme. Thinking and acting in personally meaningful ways helps you achieve excellence, contribute and stay positively motivated.

As a result, you'll avoid the rat race of doing more, wanting more, achieving more, only to realize it's really a never-ending cycle. *That's* a recipe for increasing your stress levels and experiencing negative emotions such as fear, anxiety and anger. No thanks.

Dr. Brené Brown, a bestselling author, research professor and thought leader in the areas of vulnerability, courage, worthiness and shame, talks about how we all struggle from time to time with the "never good enough" gremlins:

We are fed with a multitude of images 24/7 about every possible area of our life, including magazine ads, social media feeds, TV commercials, movies and music. It is impossible to avoid all these messages; however, it is within our power to question whether these messages are realistic, good for us, and if other alternate messages and ways of thinking are available.[15]

1. Body (Physical)

This section covers the basics of diet, exercise and adequate sleep, as well as effective breathing and mindfulness.

First let's look at some of the "whys" of taking care of our body. Estrellita Gonzalez, owner of a holistic skin care clinic, author of *Face Your Acne: 10 Holistic Ways to Eliminate Acne[16]* and parent of a teen actor, shares words that sum up why she is the Queen of Living Clean:

My number1 value is Health. If you have all the success and money in the world, it doesn't mean much when you have poor health. In my business, I see the levels of stress in people every day. It is the root of a lot of sickness and disease. We are also bombarded by the fast pace of technology and often not equipped to deal with it all. Hence, the stress becomes extreme, as do the numerous health issues that result from it. On top of all of that, we have to deal with environmental toxins and products filled with chemicals that are not only unnecessary additives, but can be bad for your health. The antidote to this, in my opinion, is we have to take care of our bodies. Period. That starts with acknowledging stress is present, a little bit of it is ok and even healthy, and it is manageable. However, too much of it should not be considered healthy, but will instead lead to problems like inflammation in the body and eventual sickness and disease. The counterbalance to stress is to manage it through lifestyle management and tools at our disposal, like regular exercise, mindfulness, yoga, meditation, eating clean, proper rest. etc.

Diet

Estrellita offers a general rule of thumb. Eat the right kinds of foods. While it's become common sense to keep junk food to a minimum and focus on getting more fruits and vegetables, there's still a lot of conflicting information about the "right kinds of foods". So where do you start and how do you avoid overcomplicating things? Estrellita offers a simple and common sense life hack:

It really starts with everyone paying attention to their gut. Use that as a guide to the state of your health. It means listening to your body. If your tummy and gut are not feeling good, don't ignore it. It is a big clue to telling you that some of the foods you are consuming are not right for you.

My golden rule for both adults and kids alike is this: if something makes you feel bad, then pay attention and take action, whether that means stopping altogether, doing it less, asking for help, or investigating further. Own it. Own yourself. You are unique. What works for you may not be what works for others, or even most others. This golden rule applies equally to your relationships with others. If someone constantly makes you feel bad somehow, then pay attention to that. It is often an important clue. Again you may have to step away from that person for good, communi-

---

15 [*] *The Gifts of Imperfection* (67-68) (Hazelden Publishing: Minnesota, 2010).

16 [*] She Power Publishing: Vancouver, 2016.

cate what you feel and try to get to a better place, or ask for help. The key is to really pay attention to how you feel and to learn to trust yourself. This self-awareness really pays off in life!

Think of food as providing fuel and the building blocks your body *needs* to build, function, heal and repair. Good stuff in, healthy body. Garbage in, garbage out. Distinguish when you're eating food for nourishment (i.e. fuel) as opposed to for pleasure or for emotional reasons. This makes you more mindful and deliberate in your food choices and portions.

A Note on Hydration

You've probably heard this life hack a million times: hydrate! There's good reason for that. There are so many benefits of drinking water, some of which are highlighted here.

- Helps combat fatigue - water IS a catalyst.
- Prevents unwanted weight gain in 2 ways: (1) calorie rich and/or non-nourishing drinks can be substituted with water or naturally flavored water and (2) the body often mistakes thirst for hunger, so you end up eating more than your body needs. So, drink more water.
- Flushes toxins from your body, so they don't accumulate, causing sickness and disease.
- Assists in keeping your skin elastic and supple – not to mention that great glow you get!
- Helps muscles and joints work better.
- Promotes heart health – lowered blood volume caused by dehydration makes even everyday activities like climbing stairs difficult.[17*]

Raj Teja and Dave Diogo, co-founders of the award-winning Canadian organic tea companies, Teaja and Garden-to-Cup, are keenly aware of these benefits and the consumer demand for healthy and interesting drink options. When you're in the mood for a refreshing alternative to plain or lemon flavored water, they suggest trying herbal teas, served hot or over ice. In the summertime, popsicles made from fruit herbal tea blends are a great treat - no sugar high or crash attached!

Exercise

When my daughter was a toddler, I went through a long and unpleasant divorce. I paid a visit to my family doctor, who I had known since I was 12. She knew I was physically active and played a lot of sports in the past, so she prescribed me a life hack I already knew about. Exercise. Exercise gets your endorphins going, which elevates your mood and produces a good feeling in your body. It's a fabulous coping mechanism, too.

---

17 * Dr. Breirley Wright, MS, RD, "6 Benefits of Staying Hydrated" (www.onemedical.com, posted August 8, 2012) and Christina Sarich "10 Essential Benefits of Drinking Water, Staying Hydrated" (www.naturalsociety.com, posted September 17, 2014).

I followed my doctor's advice, hit the gym and eventually hired a personal trainer with a background in nutrition. It was one of the best moves I made, and it inspired me to become a part-time personal trainer while my daughter was in her younger years.

Besides feeling good, you've likely experienced some of the other benefits of staying active, such as improved health, socializing and enjoyment, developing focus and skills, building confidence and enjoying nature.

As for what exercises you can do, how much, and how to stay motivated, these will vary. Here are some simple guidelines, no matter what kind of physical activity you choose to do.

Your Attitude Matters.

Take a moment to define what "fit" means to you. Resist unrealistic standards of what you should look and perform like. These lead to frustration and de-motivation Attitude is everything! Remember, being "fit" doesn't just mean being lean, strong and able to perform physical tasks. It also includes waking up every day with more energy; sleeping better; minimizing pains, aches and mood dips; and accomplishing your daily goals with focus and vitality.

Plan and Implement Until It Becomes Automatic.

Like many other things you do, exercise becomes a habit...or it doesn't. Four common reasons people don't stick to their physical activity goals are poor planning, lousy implementation, not anticipating obstacles and not dealing with those obstacles. To avoid getting derailed, build exercise into your life, prioritize it, limit screen time and find a partner in crime (e.g. friends, family members, pets) to make it more fun. Here's a smattering of activities that might fit into your life:

- Walking or biking to school
- Taking the stairs instead of the elevator
- Choosing activities that give you joy and keep you moving (e.g. dancing, martial arts, beach volleyball, tennis)
- Multi-tasking. Take a walk & talk study break with a friend. Listen to tunes during your run. Stretch while watching TV. Host your birthday at the beach volleyball facility as opposed to a sit-down place. Wash the car, clean the garage or mow the lawn.
- Staying young at heart. Play tag, capture the flag, or start a water balloon tossing competition.

Variety is the Spice of Life...and What Your Body Needs

A combination of cardiovascular, strength-building and stretching activities keeps things interesting and gives the body what it needs for optimal functioning. Online resources and apps are a great place to start. Many help you tailor your activities to your fitness level, goals and preferences. Often they require little equipment beyond comfortable clothing, running shoes and your own body weight. Sean Foy, in his book *The 10-Minute Total Body Breakthrough*[18] outlines a highly practical 10-minute total body workout called "fitness fusion," which can be done one or more times throughout the day.

- **4 minutes** of H.E.A.T. (high-energy aerobic training), which includes alternating 30 seconds of moderate activity with 30 seconds of fast activity (air boxing, jumping jacks, jogging in place, skipping, jumping lunges, burpees)
- **3 minutes** of resistance exercises (lunges, push-ups, squats)
- **2 minutes** of core-strengthening exercises (planks, abdominal crunches, back and side bridges, reverse crunches)
- **1 minute** of stretching and deep breathing (stretch muscle groups such as quadriceps, hamstrings, lats).

Sleep

In her bestselling parenting book, *The Dolphin Way*[19], psychiatrist Dr. Shimi Kang shares how paramount rest and sleep are to healing and sustaining life. She cites some of the symptoms you experience when you're exhausted and sleep deprived, such as fatigue, poor concentration and anxiety, as well as the short and long term problems that can affect your academic achievement, work and personal life:

- Weight gain brought upon by hormonal changes
- Memory and cognitive problems
- Decreased performance and alertness
- Poor quality of life, including long term problems such as high blood pressure, heart attack, obesity, psychiatric problems (depression and other mood disorders), insomnia, etc.

Dr. Kang recommends establishing a healthy sleep routine and environment in your life, one that's strong yet flexible enough to take your individual rest needs into account. Removing distractions from your sleeping area is vital. Yes, that includes your electronic devices. Sorry.

Breathing & Mindfulness

Breathing is self-explanatory, right? Maybe not as much as we think. When life throws curve balls our way, the practice of breathing calmly and rhythmically can escape us. Yet it is a powerful life hack at our disposal. As Dr. Shimi Kang points out in her book, *"Breathing deeply takes us out of the fear mode of fight, freeze or flight, and allows us to experience the awareness of choice."*[20]. She further notes *"It's simply biologically impossible to experience anxiety, panic, or anger if we're consistently breathing deeply."* You get better at it the more you practice.

---

18 [*] Workman: New York, 2009.
19 [*] Penguin Books: Toronto, 2014 (139-144).
20 [*] 125.

What's key for many is the *rhythmic* nature of breathing - maintaining a consistent ratio between the time spent on the inspiration "stroke" and the exhalation stroke. This keeps the flow in and out smooth, not choppy. Different ratios will work for different folks, though many find a longer exhalation is better.

Often the simplest technique is the easiest, which Dr. Kang explains in her book. Breathe in slowly and deeply through your nostrils, then exhale just as slowly. You can keep count, starting with a four count in and four count out and gradually increasing the count and number of breaths.

A more advanced but still easy-to-do technique is alternate nostril breathing, also referred to as "nadi shodhana." I first discovered it in an all-round wonderful app created by Dr. Ashok Gupta, called *Meaning of Life Experiment*. In this technique, you raise the index and middle finger of your right hand and rest them between your eyebrows. You then use your thumb to and ring finger to alternately close your right and left nostrils, holding your breath at the top and bottom of each breath. It sounds more complicated than it is. For a detailed description, visit The Chopra Centre's website, specifically the article called "Nadi Shodhana: How to Practice Alternate Nostril Breathing" by Melissa Eisler, a certified yoga and meditation writer and instructor.[21]*

Mindfulness practices are becoming more well-known and used. The Merriam Webster Dictionary defines mindfulness as *"the practice of maintaining a nonjudgmental state of heightened or complete awareness of one's thoughts, emotions, or experiences on a moment-to-moment basis."*[22]* Dr. Jon Kabat-Zinn, bestselling author and the founder of Mindfulness-Based Stress Reduction (MBSR) boils it down to its essence: *"Knowing what's on your mind."*[23]*

Mara St. Onge, an inspiring friend and founder of Blingja, a social enterprise business centered around teaching mindfulness, generously shares her journey for our younger readers (or parents), as well as the mindfulness practices she and her family have created and now share with schools, educators and other families.

When first I heard my friend, Vindy, was writing a book covering a variety of important topics, I felt proud and in awe of her determination. She shared tidbits of what topics she would cover and outlined the daunting task of the discipline of carving out specific times to write and work. I admired from afar, secretly glad I didn't have to get in the heads of people and do the analysis and research for what seemed to me to be an overwhelming project. Figuring out what kind of modern day issues people may be facing, researching data, collecting anecdotes, but most scary of all, reviewing your own life in order to convey empathy, understanding and share personal stories. So, you can imagine that when Vindy asked me to contribute to her book and include some instances of my youth, I had trepidations.

---

21 * http://www.chopra.com/articles/nadi-shodhana-how-to-practice-alternate-nostril-breathing.
22 * https://www.merriam-webster.com/dictionary/mindfulness.
23 * "Jon Kabat-Zinn: Defining Mindfulness" by Mindful Staff, January 11, 2017, mindful.org.

When I think of my past, the overwhelming theme of my life would have the title, "LONELI-NESS - A VERY SAD OPERA". Some of you may think you feel lonely, and that may very well be true. Even in the midst of large groups, loneliness can be felt very acutely. I can tell you that I may be able to trump you in the loneliness department. In fact, I know I can. Oh yah, I'm the queen of aloneness. I mean, if there were a President of The Lonely Hearts Club, it would hands down be me. I mean, is there even someone that is above the President? That's me. You see, I grew up on a lighthouse. Yah, not an OUTHOUSE as some people would incorrectly hear me say. A LIGHTHOUSE. You know, one of those places that's on the cover of a very sad book with the wind whipping around and you know that story is going to be about something pathetically sad. Yeah, could have been me. No brothers or sisters. Just me, my mom and step dad from the age of 8 to 16. I was lonely. It's hard to think about even though I'm an ancient person now. I didn't have any friends. I didn't have a TV. I didn't have a phone. I had books. I had my dog, Ky (the love of my life). I had my thoughts.

Ahhhhh! Thoughts! Thinking! My thoughts were my best friend and my mortal enemy. Some days I would have dark, lonely and angry thoughts. Wow, those days were tough. I could really sink into feeling sorry for myself. There was really nothing around that I could use like TV or friends that could help me get out of my head. That's when I began to realize that it is only me who that can drag myself out of these cranky moods. I remember that I used to imagine that I was somewhere else or someone else, and that I could actually pull myself out of these moods by using my thoughts to help me. I imagined that I had millions of dollars (and no parents to tell me how to spend it) and I would get carried away into my own amazing stories filled with friends, laughter and adventure. I used my own "tools" that worked for me to support my happiness health. Sometimes I would count the steps that I took. Sometimes I would take huge deep breaths and imagine I was breathing in magic happy powder and then blow out all the yucky feelings I felt in my body. Strange as it might seem these things were comforting to me. I felt "here". Or some people might say "present". I would put a clothes peg on my finger and move it randomly from digit to digit. Again, I felt "here". Each and every one of us has tools that they may not even recognize that they use to soothe anxious, angry, sad or tired feelings. What do you use?

When I eventually moved to the city to attend high school at 16, I was in a state of shock. Overwhelmed by people, noise, pollution, but most of all horrified by what I now know we call "cliques" of girls and sometime boys in my new school. I carefully observed how people behaved in groups and the conversations that were had and grew more and more confused and scared by the day.

Why did people say one thing and do another? Why did my friends talk to a person they seemed to like and then say horrible things about them behind their back? Why did everyone seem so AFRAID? Growing up in an environment where I was not judged and did not judge, I suddenly felt like a naked person standing in a glass box in the middle of the mall. What a horrible feeling. I realized that everyone around me was afraid of what everyone else thought of him or her. And for a while, so did I. I had never felt worse in my life. Oh, how I longed for my old lonely life with just my books and seagulls around me. For simplicity. But here I was. I remember saying to myself: "I can't be another person other than me." I had tried to be like some of the people I thought I admired and it never worked. In fact, I felt more "out of the group" than ever. I decided to be me. And me was fabulous. I counted my steps, dyed my hair purple, made my own club – the "Mara

Club" - and was unafraid. Oh sure, I had my moments when I allowed someone shaking their head at me or whispering to someone else to bother me, but I learned to say, "Sorry, I didn't hear you! Did you say something?", smiling of course...with my killer smile.

I realize as I have taken this past memory journey that I have taken to support Vindy in writing her book that my whole past has brought me to my present circumstances. I am now a business owner. I have a company called BLINGJA, which means to "Bling out your Inner Ninja". I teach people how to access their own personal tools to achieve solutions to problems that are both minuscule and massive. You may not believe it, but there is a solution to EVERY problem. EVERY. SINGLE. PROBLEM. I help people discover their own gift of problem solving. How to achieve "feeling good" tiny step by tiny step. One of the fundamental tool that I teach to anyone who will listen is "Blingja Breathing," a useful tool that uses guided imagery and can be used anywhere at any time.

Think of a problem or a feeling you may have: sad, overwhelmed, angry, excited, nervous, intimidated, scared. Now I want you to imagine that you are a stealth ninja dressed all in black with a mask on and you are a mindful adventurer looking for solutions to problems. You are powerful. You are in control. You have the answer. Now picture yourself at the bottom of a mountain, and you use your trusty climbing rope to pull yourself up the side of the mountain. As you do so, you take one, two, three DEEP breaths. At the top of that mountain is the most dazzling, beautiful diamond. And in that diamond is the SOLUTION. You may not know what the solution is, but you pop it into your pocket and repel back down the other side of the mountain, and as you do so, you let out that breath with a satisfying WHOOSHHHHHH. At the bottom of that mountain is a beautiful, glistening purple lake with a boat waiting there just for you to take you to the other side where you are at the bottom of the mountain (delete: again) and you start again.

And you are powerful.

2. *Mind (Intellectual)*

Becoming a student of life is a sure fire way of exercising your mind every day, building a great career and enjoying life fully. Later in the book, I expand on how to do this, like cultivating your strengths, taking on challenges, becoming a curious adventurer and more!

3. *Heart and Soul (Emotional and Spiritual)*

Peace is joy at rest
Joy is peace in action
- Unknown

Earlier, we discussed cultivating a loving attitude. We talked about using a gratitude journal and listing your victories, as well as using key words and practicing actions that help build stronger relationships. Strong relationships naturally nourish the heart and soul. Later in the book, we cover the topics of giving back, as well as engaging in play, both of which feed the heart and soul.

There are also other powerful and deeply spiritual activities which feed the soul and body, such as meditation and prayer. They can help lower your stress levels, thereby lowering the risk of illness or helping to manage it. They also help develop your resilience, the ability to overcome adversity in your life.

Spirituality does not necessarily involve religion. Rather, it's about a shared and deeply held belief. Dr. Brené Brown, author of *The Gifts of Imperfection*, offers an excellent definition of "spirituality":

Spirituality is recognizing and celebrating that we are all inextricably connected to each other by a power greater than all of us, and that our connection to that power and to one another is grounded in love and compassion. Practicing spirituality brings a sense of perspective, meaning and purpose to our lives.[24] *

Suzanne Pelletier, a parent, social work school graduate and one of the kindest and funniest people I know, offers a unique spiritual perspective. Suzanne and I met when she was a UWO law student and I was serving as the Director of Career Development. During her time there, she developed a serious illness which caused her to end her law school studies. She had to re-think her whole life, not to mention her career goals. Her health journey has taught her some important spiritual lessons.

What I came to understand is that peace is the starting point for so much in life. When you want to improve anything, it all starts with peace. Without peace within, it's difficult to connect genuinely or well with others, or feel true enjoyment while doing something. People who cause a lot of pain to themselves and others often do it because they lack the peace within themselves.

Feeling and practicing the triad of love, joy and peace has allowed me to simplify my life in a way many people struggle to do so all their lives. Because of my condition and the damage to my body, I live in physical pain. However, when I experience moments of pain-free living and can truly enjoy all that is good in my life, I am so grateful for being at peace that I can't even talk about it. It's that powerful for me!

Spirituality can also help you get through the tough times by giving you meaning, perspective and purpose, without resorting to self-destructive addictions such as drugs, alcohol, gambling, pornography, food or overspending. There's no doubt you've dealt with, or will have to deal with, unpleasant situations in your life. These might include illness or injuries, bullies at school or online, job or financial struggles, loss of loved ones, struggling relationships, family conflict and so on. Spirituality can be a welcomed friend at these times. It can offer a healthy escape, confidence boost, and sense of peace when you badly need it.

I did a lot of soul searching when I was going through what turned out to be a grueling divorce. There were so many changes to manage – legal, financial, parenting, emotional and social. Grey hairs were popping out all over my head! Though religion was not a big part of my upbringing, I recall my grandmother reciting Sikh religious hymns every morning. During the divorce, my cousin Arv gave me a book containing those hymns and their English translations. It was the perfect gift at the perfect time.

---

24 * Hazelden Publishing: Minnesota, 2010.

Reciting those hymns helped quiet my mind, and I temporarily suspended thoughts about my never-ending Divorce To Do list. I developed a habit of listening to them on my device while I rollerbladed ten kilometers around Vancouver's gorgeous Stanley Park. The combination of prayer, nature and physical exercise was my solace. My personal life hack. It helped me disconnect, so I could reconnect more effectively. During my walks and drives now, I like to tune into Oprah Winfrey's *SuperSoul Conversations* podcast for thirty-minute doses of spirituality and inspiration.

Another positive practice I found through Randy Purcell and Kjirsten Sigmund of Meditate Vancouver[25], is Metta Meditation. It's also referred to as "Loving Kindness Meditation." I usually do it in the mornings for about fifteen to twenty minutes and at night if I'm disciplined enough. It uses ancient wisdom, neuroscience, heart coherence and quantum physics to master the Power of Love. If you're like me and traditional meditation is challenging, or if you struggle with "monkey mind" during meditation (your thoughts continue to drift here, there and everywhere), this might be a fantastic option. It gives your mind something *to do* during meditation. You start with ten grounding breaths, six count in and ten count out. This usually takes about two to three minutes. Then you start the Metta Process Stage 1.

You think of someone dear to you. Then you deeply feel these five wishes for them.

1 May you be happy
2 May you be safe
3 May you be healthy and strong
4 May you awaken to the light of your true nature
5 May you live with ease

You make these five wishes for all of the following:

- Someone close to you (family or friends)
- Yourself (designed to heal and increase self-acceptance and lessen self-criticism)
- Someone you know in passing (a neighbor you see but don't know, a clerk at local grocery store)
- Someone you're having or had difficulty with (this one may be hard to do but essential to the practice)
- Entire planet

Metta Process Stage 2 is more advanced and invites you to focus on three ideals and emotions:

- Impartiality (imagining loving those you don't know as deeply as those close to you)
- Compassion (imagining people or groups you believe are suffering, and wish for their suffering to end)
- Joy in the good fortune of others (being genuinely happy for those feeling joy or experiencing good fortune)

A lot of people deal with family and relationship dysfunction, so this meditation may be a very new way of experiencing the world. The steps are easier said than done. But remember it is a moment by moment practice. The simplicity and depth of Metta Meditation practice is a very powerful combination if you want to increase your life satisfaction as well as your positive emotions.

---

25 * www.meditatevancouver.com.

Chapter 6: Actions - Practicing Self Care

Life Hacks

Body (Physical)

1. *Diet. Eat a balance of foods and stay hydrated. If your tummy and gut are not feeling good, some of the foods you're consuming might not be right for you. Become more mindful by distinguishing when you're eating for nourishment vs for pleasure or emotional reasons.*

2. *Exercise.*
   a. *Resist unrealistic standards. Fit includes sleeping better; minimizing pains, aches and mood dips; and accomplishing daily goals with focus and vitality.*
   b. *Plan and implement until it becomes automatic. Build exercise into your life, prioritize it, limit screen time and if it helps, find a partner to make it more fun.*
   c. *A combination of cardiovascular, strength-building and stretch activities keeps things interesting and gives the body what it needs for optimal functioning.*

3. *Sleep. Rest and sleep are necessary for healing and sustaining life. Establish a healthy sleep routine and environment, one that's strong yet flexible enough to take your individual rest needs into account.*

4. *Breathing & Mindfulness. Breathing deeply takes you out of the fear mode of fight, freeze or flight, and therefore allows you to experience the awareness of choice. Mindfulness refers to the practice of maintaining a nonjudgmental state of heightened or awareness of your thoughts, emotions, or experiences on a moment-to-moment basis.*

Mind (Intellectual). Becoming a student of life is a sure fire way of exercising your mind continually, building a great career and enjoying life fully.

Heart and Soul (Emotional and Spiritual). Spirituality is a shared and deeply held belief (does not necessarily involve religion) that can ground you, and also help you get through tough times by giving you meaning, perspective and purpose, without resorting to self-destructive addictions.

Questions and Exercises

1. Once you've reviewed the basics of self-care in this chapter, consider your own self-care regime closely. What things can you add or tweak, without feeling overwhelmed?

2. Which self-care ideas make the most sense to you? If you have a long list of ideas, prioritize them according to your needs, current health, and future goals.

3. If you're unsure about how to go about implementing changes, who can you ask for help (friend, family member, health care provider, Dr. Google)?

Notes

Notes

SECTION B: COURAGE

CHAPTER SEVEN

COURAGE - STAND UP FOR WHAT YOU BELIEVE IN

True courage is in facing danger when you are afraid...
— L. Frank Baum, The Wonderful Wizard of Oz

1. *What is Courage?*

Courage is strength in the face of fear, pain and/or grief. It doesn't mean you deny those emotions. It means you speak or act in spite of them. For example, you have the courage to not ignore certain distressing information and further, the ability to absorb and process that information. You have the courage to say and do things that may be mistakes, make you look uncomfortable or foolish, cause conflict, or upset the status quo. Read those last two sentences again. Sounds like a good time, doesn't it? Not. There'd better be good reasons for developing and practicing courage, right?

Peter Mwariga describes courage as something often associated with surviving some kind of trauma and developing resilience as a result. In that difficult place, whatever challenge it migh be, we are shaped. Obviously not everyone has to go through trauma to be courageous. After all, trauma is an experience you have that overwhelms your capacity to cope. Some people are naturally courageous. However, this quality usually only shows when it's measured against a challenge that person is facing. Here's how Peter helps his coaching clients who are struggling with a serious challenge:

I encourage them to look back into their lives and find something significant that marks a point when they were courageous. It could be anything. The time they were young, learning to swim, had to jump off the diving board and were petrified to do it. Once they did it, or even decided they could do it, they overcame their mental block. Then when they look at the challenge, it looks softer and far less intimidating.

2. *Life Shrinks or Expands in Proportion to One's Courage.*

Life can be busy and full of competing demands from partners, bosses/teachers, family members and friends. On top of that, you have your own thoughts and plans. Giving into the demands of others all the time robs you of your initiative, independence and, ultimately, your satisfaction. However, the flip side is not a bed of roses either. Constantly demanding others to do what you want makes you inflexible, uncooperative and a pain to be around.

There must be a middle ground which helps you build strong relationships, have fun and work towards your goals? The middle ground is not the same as "getting by." That's managing, not flourishing. The middle ground involves practicing courage. That means having the courage to face and deal with life's uncertainties, conflicts and obstacles. It also means having the courage to say "no" to the things that do not fit your values[26*] so you can say "yes" to those that do.

In the absence of courage, there's avoidance. Avoiding or running away from problems doesn't mean they disappear. In fact, they may just get worse, less manageable, or paralyze you into doing nothing. So while it's true that playing it safe may prevent you from getting hurt or disappointed *some of the time*, it also encourages you to stay stuck, watching from the sidelines of life *a lot of the time*. The missing link is courage.

Let's consider a simple and classic bullying example to illustrate these points about courage.

Rick is bullying Tara. Their English professor in college chose them, along with two other classmates (Nicole and Dylan), to represent the school in an upcoming inter-school speech competition. Tara had a tough time in high school and was teased a lot. She's worked hard on building her confidence and taking on new challenges, like public speaking, and is favored to win the competition. Rick really wants to clinch this competition, because he's sure it'll help him increase his chances to get into law school. Using various social media sites under a pseudonym, Rick has been taking low blows at Tara, seriously embarrassing her and affecting her confidence. She's having bad flashbacks to her high school days. Rick's friend Dave, who is also in the English class, helped him set up the fake accounts.

Tara approaches Rick and Dave, but they deny any wrongdoing. Several other classmates are also now aware of Rick's actions, including Nicole and Dylan, the other two competitors. Nicole decides to say nothing to the professor or to Rick and Dave. She feels really bad for Tara, and though she doesn't really care if Tara beats her or not, she chooses not to act. Dylan encourages Tara to go with him to report the incident to the professor, but she's resistant. Rick and Dave intimidate her. Dylan approaches the two men and they deny having anything to do with the online bullying. Dylan decides to report it to the professor anyways. The end result: the professor verifies the bad behavior and withdraws Rick from the competition. He and Dave also face other serious academic consequences. Tara ultimately wins the speech competition.

Let's identify the roles in this scenario, to see how courage in action works.

Tara is the Victim. She's intentionally targeted. She exercises the courage to approach and question Rick and Dave.

Rick is the Perpetrator. His desire to get into the law school does not in any way excuse his unethical and damaging actions.

Dave is the Enabler. He's knowingly helping Rick do something harmful. He lacks the courage to say "no", even if his personal values may not align with Rick's. He has nothing to gain directly, except perhaps a stronger friendship with Rick and a future favor from him.

---

26 * For a helpful exercise on identifying, grouping, and narrowing down your values, see https://www.cmu.edu/career/documents/my-career-path-activities/values-exercise.pdf

Nicole is the Bystander. She's aware of the wrongdoing and does nothing about it. Though she feels bad for Tara and has no ill motive, she chooses to do nothing. She misses an opportunity to exercise courage, and potentially stays stuck in her passivity.

Dylan is an Upstander. He's aware of the bad behavior and does something about it. He loses the speech competition, but acts with integrity and courage.

Flexing your courage muscle can result in some cuts and bruises along the way. However, this life hack allows you to strengthen yourself internally. You'll discover your real self, abilities and true passions. Externally, you'll notice your relationships with others become more honest, open and stronger. Why? Courage allows you to take small risks along the way, build trust and make natural gains along the journey.

3. *Say What You Mean and Mean What You Say*

Earlier, the spotlight was on the power of words to shape actions and techniques to accomplish this: substituting harsher words with kinder ones, listening more and asking a lot of questions. Not only do these techniques build your courage muscles faster, they enhance your ability to say what you mean and mean what you say.

You might be thinking that sounds too good to be true. After all, it's easy to misunderstand what others say, and vice versa. It happens all the time. A handy life hack here is the Diamond Communication Method, as I like to call it. Dal Sohal, a university instructor, leadership consultant and coach with PAIRS consulting, introduced me to this method.

Picture a baseball diamond. Break down "say what you mean" into four bases, or steps, which allows you to think and communicate clearly:

1. *I notice...*
2. *I think...*
3. *I feel...*
4. *I want...*

Stop at each base and speak from there. For example:

1. I notice you slammed the door earlier when you went upstairs, after we discussed the weekend plans.

2. That makes me think you might be upset or angry with me.

3. I feel frustrated that this keeps happening.

4. I want us to talk about our plans in a calmer way or for you to let me know when something bothers you. And I want us to reach an agreement about our plans, or at least agree to disagree about what we want to do.

The last step is the one that often gets missed. You might hesitate to ask for what you want for any number of reasons. You're afraid of rejection, have no clue what answer you might hear, or think it's obvious what you want and the other person knows, or should know. However, the last step of asking for what you want affords you a chance to strengthen your communication and relationship, avoid misunderstandings and prevent the likelihood of similar future conflicts.

This technique comes in handy when you're tempted to react emotionally. The baseball diamond visual helps you walk through the four steps, clarify your thinking, obtain any relevant or missing information, get clear on what you really want, and share that with the other person.

You feel more real when you say what you mean and mean what you say, particularly in close relationships. You won't be agreeable or be a chameleon when it's not necessary or compromises who you are. When referring to a human being, a chameleon refers to a person who shifts their behavior or opinions depending on the situation. Aside from actors, chameleons are usually not respected, liked or considered trustworthy, because they're self-serving and seem to shift their values continuously.

Chapter 7: Courage - Stand Up For What You Believe In

Life Hacks

Courage is strength in the face of fear, pain and/or grief. You don't deny those emotions, but you speak or act in spite of them.

Life shrinks or expands in proportion to one's courage. You build stronger relationships, have more fun and work more effectively towards your goals when you (1) have the courage to face and deal with life's uncertainties, conflicts and obstacles, and (2) have the courage to say "no" to the things that do not fit your values so you can say "yes" to those that do.

In the absence of courage, there is avoidance. Avoiding or running away from problems doesn't mean they disappear. In fact, they may just get worse, less manageable, or paralyze you into doing nothing.

Say what you mean, and mean what you say. To avoid misunderstanding what others say and do, and vice versa, try the Diamond Communication Method. Break down what you say into four steps, allowing you to think and communicate clearly: (1) "I notice..." (2) "I think..." (3) "I feel..." (4) "I want...

Questions and Exercises

1. Pinpoint a situation or relationship in which you faced uncertainty, conflict, or obstacles with courage, or had the courage to say "no" to something that didn't align with your values. What did you do? What did you say? How did it feel? What were the short term and long term results?

2. Now think of a situation or relationships in which you practiced avoidance, whether it was intentional or not. What were the short term and long term results? If faced with the same circumstances, what would you do the same? Differently?

3. Practice using the Diamond Communication Method with family and friends. You may find it helpful to write out what you're going to say, or to role play it with someone, until it feels more natural to move through the steps.

Notes

Notes

CHAPTER EIGHT

COURAGE - THE HOW TOS

Obstacles don't have to stop you. If you run into a wall, don't turn around and give up. Figure out how to climb it, go through it, or work around it.

\- Michael Jordan, retired NBA player and superstar

Living courageously rewards you with a ton of learning, growth and opportunity, yet many still shy away from it. Many years ago, my friend Bill Inman, introduced me to a practical way of moving past this reluctance. He said, *"Understand the obstacles you face and develop a different, more productive mindset around how to approach them.* This is a dynamic way to develop your courage capacity.

Over the years I've expanded upon that handy life hack. Though these tips may not translate into daily habits automatically, they become more second nature with practice.

1. *Replace Fear with Focus*

Fear

It's important to distinguish how the terms "fear" and "danger" are used here. Danger is real. It's the real possibility of suffering harm or injury, and such threats and risks need to be dealt with. Fears live mainly in your head and heart, though not always. That makes them real, at least for you and others who share them.

You will not be shocked to hear there are probably more fears out there than ice cream flavors. Do you recognize any that have shown up in your life or someone you care about?

- Fear of conflict
- Fear of criticism or punishment
- Fear of rejection
- Fear of failure
- Fear of disappointment
- Fear of being miserable
- Fear of loneliness
- Fear of the unknown

And the list goes on. You may experience them on a daily, weekly, monthly and yearly basis! Lucky for you, there's no age exemption either. Conquering your fears helps you to not only function in life, but also to flourish. Most of us don't just want to get by. We want to experience life more fully. That means you have to deal with some or all of your fears.

Recently, I faced my fear about "putting myself out there" and applied to be a TEDx speaker. I was passionate about the idea I wanted to share, that premarital agreements (commonly known as prenups) not only help people protect financial assets, but also decrease divorce stress as well as strengthen relationships, before and during marriage. Not only was I a bit freaked out about putting myself on the world stage, I knew I'd be sharing parts of my personal story. I'm not going to lie. I had an assortment of fears. But I did it. I threw myself into the application process, successfully landed an interview and was chosen as a speaker! This gave me an amazing platform to potentially help a lot of people shift their thinking, and improve their lives.

Review the list of fears again, and then consider the equally long list of benefits that come with putting your fears to rest:

- Fears limit or even stop you from trying new things, exploring different solutions and discovering new things about yourself and the world. Fears are really opportunities for growth and learning.

- Conflict is a normal part of life, and conflict resolution is a valuable life skill, acquired with time and practice.

- Agreeing, passively accepting things, or "faking it" are often unnecessary or may compromise who you are. Sometimes you have to disappoint others to stay true to yourself.

- Fears sometimes hold you back from protecting yourself and those you care about, leaving you damaged in some way or feeling powerless and insecure.

- Fears encourage you to make assumptions, take things personally and generally "play a movie" in your head, which may not even be accurate.

- Opening up and communicating certain things can be really difficult. A close friend or family member may misinterpret or use something against you. Unfortunately, that's the person's choice, and maybe you aren't able to reasonably predict their reaction. But the potential payoff for risking that vulnerability in important relationships can be amazing. You risk it...for love. It's also part of choosing deeper and more meaningful connections in your life over superficial ones.

- Feelings of fear are just messages you get from your brain and nervous system. They're a normal part of life, and what you do with them is what matters. Ignoring them altogether can lead to bad outcomes. On the other hand, allowing them to dominate your thoughts and actions often makes things much worse.

- To get along with others and even love them, you don't have to agree with everything they do or believe.

During his years playing as a competitive ice and ball hockey goalie, and later coaching his son's ice hockey teams, Larry Beryar discovered you often have to experience failure or doubt to really know or appreciate success.

As a goalie, he learned that to focus and play well, it was critical to believe in himself on the one hand and manage his fear of failure on the other. He found that great players are often motivated by self-confidence and the need to prove themselves, as well as the need to show they could perform in the face of fear.

This all hit home in the locker room right before a Canadian Ball Hockey Championship game, where he was surprised to see a much more experienced star rival goalie throw up owing to pre-game nerves. Once Larry became a seasoned goalie himself, he realized those nerves were completely natural. Once you're a top goalie, you have a reputation to uphold and protect, not to mention a team that relies heavily on you. The best and worst thing to hear from teammates was. *"Don't worry, we have Larry in goal."* Everybody sees your mistakes: shots saved vs. shots not saved. You quickly learn you can't be invincible.

Many years later, as a hockey coach to his son's teams, he strove to teach his players the importance of knowing failure to appreciate success, pointing out what they learn about themselves and others during this process. In fact, he often shared this quote with the kids, from the late great world championship boxer Mohammed Ali:

Only the man who knows what it is like to be defeated can reach down to the bottom of his soul and come up with the extra ounce of power it takes to win when the match is even.

When you find a fear threatening to paralyze you from moving forward, keep this acronym in mind:

F – False

E – Evidence

A – Appearing

R – Real

Focus

Focus is a highly effective "cure" to fear and worry. It's also like a muscle, which gets stronger the more you exercise it. When you bring focus to any situation, you automatically zero in on what's important and why, rather than worrying about what may or may not happen afterwards.

Take an interpersonal conflict as an example. Focusing allows you to do four main things:

- Figure out what you're thinking and feeling *(self-awareness)*.
- Determine how to conduct yourself based on who you are, your values and your goals *(self-controlling/self-management)*.
- Consider the other person's perspective and place *(awareness of other)*.
- Resolve the matter using the appropriate communication techniques and/or actions *(relationship management)*.

Don't get me wrong. Situations are not always resolved to your satisfaction. You may experience disappointment, sadness, or frustration if you don't get the outcome you want. However, with this life hack, you're moving forward one step at a time using your thoughts, words and actions, rather than being paralyzed by fear.

2. *Replace Guilt with Intention*

Guilt

Guilt is often an unproductive emotion, particularly when you haven't intended to do or say anything wrong or hurtful. Recall a time when you gave up something you considered valuable, or went out of your way because you felt guilty about disappointing someone or hurting their feelings. You may have even suffered in silence to protect the other.

Here's the dilemma. Kindness, empathy and compassion are positive traits to cultivate. Demonstrating them strengthens your relationships. On the other hand, staying true to yourself and respecting your own needs and wants affects your growth as well as the strength and honesty of your relationships. Balancing these principles and dealing with your feelings of guilt head on can help grow your relationships. However, if your feelings of guilt lead you to abandon or seriously compromise your own values and goals, you risk becoming withdrawn, resentful, or fake. This can ultimately lead to far more problems than it solves in the short term!

Let's take a scenario.

Susan is considered the "responsible one" among her adult siblings. Her parents have confidence in her, often giving her additional responsibilities. She feels guilty voicing her objections because her mom and dad have busy lives and have devoted a lot of time and money supporting her education and career goals. Susan enjoys doing things for them but feels she doesn't get a break and often lacks the time to complete her own household chores.

Over time, Susan resents her brother and sister for not volunteering their time, but is reluctant to voice her concerns for fear of hurting their feelings. Fast forward a few years. The short term gains of pleasing her parents and protecting her siblings' feelings are now replaced with the longer term pain that comes from an unsatisfying and closed relationship with her parents and siblings, as well diminished awareness and motivation to pursue her own passions and interests. Not a pretty picture.

Intention

My mom gave me her own two-step life hack on how to combat guilt with intention. Firstly, she stressed that it's important to be present and aware. That way, you know *why* you are saying "yes" or "no" to something or someone. Secondly, you need to understand what your priorities are, based on your values, and who is really important to you. Once you do those things, you can better balance these priorities and key relationships with other responsibilities and requests that come your way.

Without thinking about both steps, it's too easy to have thoughts and actions dictated *to* you. After all, others tend to operate from their own agendas. They may be unaware of your feelings or other obligations. It's possible they may not even care, because they're too absorbed or stressed out with their own lives. Your *intention* – what YOU want - becomes central to your decision-making. If it is not negative or intended to harm the other person, you're more likely to speak up or offer other suggestions.

Using our Susan the Responsible One as the example, it would be useful for Susan to check in with herself to know what's on her plate and her own energy limits then reach a better compromise if possible. Her intention is not to burden her parents, but to strike a balance. This alleviates the feeling of guilt associated with saying "no" or "not yet".

3. Replace Doubt with Confidence

Doubt

Doubt gets in the way of practicing courage. Doubt is a feeling of uncertainty, hesitation or confusion. When you have doubts, you second guess yourself. That often leads to giving up too easily and not even acting or speaking up in the first place. The negative effect is the same as guilt and fear. Doubt doesn't serve us well.

Confidence

Self-doubt lessens gradually when you replace it with confidence. Confidence is a feeling of self-assurance or certainty that comes from knowing, appreciating and trusting your abilities and qualities.[27]

It doesn't have to be loud or in your face. It can be quiet and certain. And it's a life hack that keeps paying off.

Though many seem to exude natural confidence, this quality can easily be acquired and fortified with knowledge and experience. As long as you take time to understand yourself, reflect and continually engage with the world, you'll be supplied with steady opportunities to build your confidence. Parts 2 and 3 of the book expand on these opportunities.

---

27 * Oxford Live Dictionaries. https://en.oxforddictionaries.com/definition/confidence.

Chapter 8: Courage - The How Tos

Life Hacks

Replace fear with focus. Fears, though not always, live mainly in your head and heart. Conquering them comes with many advantages, including growth, learning, staying true to yourself, deeper relationships and fewer insecurities or feelings of powerlessness. When you bring focus to any situation, you zero in on what's important and why. Focus leads to better self-awareness, self-management, awareness of other and relationship management.

Replace Guilt with Intention. Guilt is often unproductive. When it leads you to compromise your own values and goals, you risk becoming withdrawn, resentful, or fake. This can ultimately lead to more problems than it solves in any relationship. Be present and aware instead. That way, you know why you are saying "yes" or "no" to something or someone. Secondly, understand what your priorities are (based on your values), and who is important to you. When you are intentional this way, you can make more balanced choices.

Replace Doubt with Confidence. Doubt gets in the way of practicing courage. Doubt is a feeling of uncertainty, hesitation or confusion. Confidence is a feeling of self-assurance or certainty that comes from trusting, appreciating and knowing your abilities and qualities. This quality occurs naturally, but can also be acquired and strengthened with knowledge and experience.

Questions and Exercises

1. What are some fears that you've dealt with successfully in your life or relationships? What benefits have you enjoyed as a result of putting them to rest? What role did **focus** play in helping you navigate and resolve situations?

2. Recall times when you gave up something you considered valuable and had genuine regrets about doing so, or went out of your way because you felt guilty about disappointing someone or hurting their feelings. Did you end up disappointing yourself or others in the process? Were any of your personal values compromised? If so, how would you do things differently if faced with similar circumstances?

3. Which areas of your life do you feel confident in? In what areas would you like to experience more confidence...or just some confidence period?! What opportunities could you pursue to gain some knowledge in these areas?

SECTION C: WISDOM

CHAPTER NINE

WHY WISDOM?

Everything that irritates us about others can lead us to an understanding of ourselves.
- Carl Jung

You attract people with the qualities you display, you keep them with the qualities you possess.
- Unknown

The truth will set you free. But first it will piss you off.
- Gloria Steinem

1. *Naked Relationships*

Wisdom refers to the quality of having experience, knowledge and good judgement.

Naked relationships requires wisdom. Naked relationships? What kind of book is this? It's not as bad as it sounds. Actually it's not bad at all. It might be the most transformative life hacks you'll come across. Naked relationships are those characterized by open and honest communication, ones in which you try to know and accept each other, warts and all. It also means telling the truth, even when it hurts or might get you in trouble. It doesn't mean sharing every single thing about yourself and vice versa. After all, it takes time, trust and experience to get to know someone really well, even your own family members. However, if we're always holding back, our most valued relationships don't get a chance to develop depth.

"Naked relationships begin with cultivating that concept within yourself," says Peter Mwariga. Peter thinks this starts with a willingness to accept yourself and peel back the layers of the onion to the point that you're comfortable with yourself. This prepares you for having more honest relationships with others. When Peter was doing his coaching certification, one of the key "tests" students were encouraged to ask themselves is, *"Are you being authentic with yourself?"* Like relationships, this is an ongoing process, in which you become more comfortable and authentic with yourself over time.

Peter adds a caveat:

Don't get me wrong. Naked, bold and open is not a ticket to being rude and insensitive. You have to protect yourself while simultaneously passing the message along. It's a balancing act. Sometimes it's important to protect the other person and hold back the message. At other times, it's absolutely necessary to speak up. The key question I always ask myself is this: 'Is this going to move us forward or backward? Ask yourself that question each time you're in doubt.

Generally, people shut down if they feel they're under attack. If I act combative, and so does the other person, all claiming to be 'naked in their relationships,' you'll soon have a war. Not surprisingly, this again all starts with the individual. You have to learn that balancing act within yourself. If you get up every morning and bombard yourself with hard truths every morning – I didn't do errands, I didn't finish my work, I wasn't nice to my friend yesterday – then you would crawl back into your bed and never leave the house! You have to be compassionate and forgiving with yourself, and that allows you to do it with others.

2. *Handling Information Properly*

Wisdom gives you an edge...the ability to handle information appropriately. It helps you directly affect outcomes. Practicing it showcases your best self. You build relationships where you're not only safe to be yourself, you allow and encourage others to do the same. Think of wisdom as the proverbial magic wand that boosts the quality of your life.

Consider the example of Ariana, Soo-Lin, and a high school talent show.

Ariana asks her friend Soo-Lin to sign her up for the talent show while she's at a dental appointment. Soo-Lin agrees. Ariana later learns that Soo-Lin missed the deadline and is upset with her, not to mention the disappointment she feels about missing an opportunity to do something fun and make new friends. She transferred in the 10th grade to a new school, and it's been tough making new friends. Ariana fears confronting Soo-Lin because Soo-Lin has been the kindest friend she's had all year at the new school and doesn't want her to take her disappointment the wrong way. How should Ariana handle the information?

3. *Love, Courage and Wisdom in Action*

Love, Courage and Wisdom to the rescue. Love allows Ariana to reflect on the importance of her friendship with Soo-Lin.

Courage allows her to overcome her fears and replace them with focus. Focus includes checking in with her feelings (upset and disappointed), contemplating what Soo-Lin is like (thoughtful), deciding what she'd like to accomplish (find out what happened and know whether she can or should rely on her friend in the future) and figuring out how to do all this (have a conversation).

Wisdom guides Ariana through the situation so she handles information without ignoring her own feelings, nor making them the be all and end all. Ariana gave up friends she had known since grade school when she moved. She knows strong friendships require trust building, which takes time and risks. Ariana asks questions, gives Soo-Lin an opportunity to explain her side, and listens with an open mind. She realizes she genuinely likes Soo-Lin, but hasn't known her for a long time. She had no idea Soo-Lin was busy with so many extra-curricular activities plus a part time job at the library.

Soo-Lin knew Ariana was pretty new to the school and leaned on her, but on the day of sign-up, Soo-Lin had been called into work when someone called in sick. She forgot to text Ariana and the teacher coordinating the show. Ariana, in turn, shares why the missed chance affected her. Sharing information usually increases the mutual understanding between friends, as it did in this scenario. In other cases, it may expose genuine gaps that make a close relationship problematic or even impossible.

Ariana concludes that Soo-Lin didn't mean any harm and that it's unlikely to happen again. But she's also motivated to expand her social circle, in part so Soo-Lin doesn't feel pressure to "look after" Ariana. Soo-Lin regrets what happened and offers to talk to the organizing teacher to see if anything can be done. Gradually these two young women make gains in their friendship.

Imagine if Ariana just stewed about the whole thing and never approached Soo-Lin to get clarification. That happens way more than it should, with kids and adults alike. Or worse, what if Ariana actually took out her frustration out on Soo-Lin without first getting more information. That also happens too often.

While wisdom is not an actual magic wand, practicing it definitely has the power to improve lives and relationships immeasurably, even miraculously.

Chapter 9: Why Wisdom?

Life Hacks

Seek "naked relationships", including with yourself. Naked relationships are those characerized by open and honest communication, ones in which you try to know and accept each other, warts and all. It also means telling the truth, even when it hurts or might get you in trouble.

Wisdom gives you the ability to handle information appropriately. It helps you directly affect situation outcomes. Practicing it showcases your best self, allows you to build relationships where you are safe to be yourself, and allow others to do the same.

Love, courage and wisdom works together. Love prompts you to reflect on the importance of a relationship or situation. Courage allows you to overcome your fears and replace them with focus. Wisdom can guide you through a situation so you handle information without ignoring your own feelings, nor making them the be all and end all.

Questions and Exercises

1. Consider which relationships in your life are "naked". What positive qualities do you or the other person tend to exhibit? How can you incorporate these qualities into relationships you'd like to see become more open and honest?

2. Think of a time when you handled information in a way that lead to a positive outcome, or avoided a potentially negative one. What did you learn? How did it impact your views about relationship building, trust, discretion or open-mindedness?

3. Now flip the scenario in Question #2. Think of a time when you think you could have handled information differently? If presented with this scenario again, what would you do?

Notes

Notes

CHAPTER TEN

WISDOM 101 - BASIC CONCEPTS

When you become comfortable with uncertainty, infinite possibilities open up in your life.
- Eckhart Tolle

Pay attention to whether your energy increases or decreases when you're around certain people. That's the universe's way of telling you who you should stay close to and who you should get away from.
- Unknown

Appreciating what wisdom constitutes and why it's applicable to your day-to-day life is the perfect set up to introducing practical concepts you can apply in your wisdom journey.

1. *Embracing and Learning From Differences*

When something or someone is different or unfamiliar, you may find yourself guarded, rather than curious or open. Sometimes this is for legitimate reasons, such as safety (yours and/or others') or negative past experiences. Other times, you may feel your "energy state" affected. Dr. Rupinder Toor, a parent, women's health practitioner, as well as Founder and Director of Northeast Calgary Women's Clinic, regularly invokes the energy quote above, describing her general rule of thumb this way:

For example, certain activities you do or people you are around make you feel energized and leave you excited afterwards. You're buzzed from it. Continue to put your positive efforts into these things and folks. And then, there are other things or people who leave you feeling down, demotivated, lethargic. Pay attention to this. Avoid these things or people if you can.

Jonathan Michael, the expert in The Birkman Method, adds another dimension to this concept. He explains that embracing and learning from differences does not necessarily equal the following:

- Adopting others' values
- Agreeing with everything or most of what they do or believe
- Approving of who they are and what they do
- Even liking or loving them

After all, you don't have to be best friends with someone to embrace and learn from them. You also don't have to fear or hate those whose lifestyle you disagree with. When you simply lack a reason for being on guard other than your own fear, mostly fear of the unknown, you put up a roadblock in your wisdom journeys. In other words, you might miss chances to expand your understanding of yourselves, others and the world.

Many of the world's most respected leaders and peacemakers of the past, were also experts in learning from and embracing differences. Think about Nelson Mandela, Mohandas Gandhi, Mother Theresa and Martin Luther King, Jr. All were revered for their keen understanding of the universal human condition, dedication and problem solving abilities. This helped them make a lasting and positive difference in their communities and around the world.

2. A Little Compassion and Understanding Go a LONG Way

When you show compassion and understanding to others, they're less likely to feel threatened by you, more likely to open up and be honest with you, and more willing to share their ideas with you. Co-operative solutions come from this safe place.

The opposite usually comes from insisting on "your way or the highway," assuming the worst, or accusing others of bad motives. You may get your way in the short-term, but the long term damage to the relationship hardly makes it worth it.

3. When to Speak Up, Back Down, or Just Stay Silent

The ability to speak several languages is an asset, but the ability to keep your mouth shut in any language is priceless.
- Unknown

I stopped explaining myself when I realized people only understand from their level of perception.
- Spirit Science

Discretion refers to having the freedom to decide what to say or do in a given situation. Wisdom gives you the ability to handle information appropriately. Using your wisdom while exercising your discretion allows you to do one or many of the following:

- Figure out what's necessary or best to share
- Speak up now or later
- Back down permanently, until a later time, or until circumstances change
- Stay silent
- Take a certain course of action

All these choices may seem overwhelming. Humans tend to love certainty, but often you don't know the answers and lack evidence suggesting clear answers. The life hack here is simple but powerful. There's *always* something you can do, even if you're in the darkest place. It may be an internal shift or an external action.

For example, you may find yourself in a difficult situation or friendship. You're trying to be compassionate and helpful, but your friend consistently puts her needs first and demonstrates a lack empathy for you. You may even know your friend suffers from serious insecurities, and you feel bad for her. Knowingly or unknowingly, these insecurities motivate her to consistently act in a way that's self-serving but harmful to others. When you finally muster the courage to confront her with all of this, she claims to be the victim. She may be oblivious to her own behavior...or be unable or unwilling to face what she's doing. As one of the quotes at the beginning of this chapter suggests, she may simply lack the knowledge and maturity to understand what you're trying to communicate.

Walking away from such a relationship or situation may be your healthiest option. At the very least, you're better served if you adjust your attitudes about her or insist on stronger boundaries. No matter how caring and evolved you are, it's important to accept when a situation is simply not working. This prompts you to limit its presence and importance in your life, freeing you to focus on activities and relationships that reflect more of your true self. Not only is this an act of self-respect, it's also wisdom in action!

Acquiring wisdom is not simple or automatic. It's a life-long process. It includes making your own mistakes and learning from them, as well as becoming keen observers of life. It also involves seeking wisdom from those you respect, such as trusted family members, friends, spiritual leaders, teachers, coaches, authors and speakers. Gradually, you learn to exercise your own discretion effectively and gain your own individual brand of wisdom.

Chapter 10: Wisdom 101 - Basic Concepts

Life Hacks

:mbrace and learn from differences. When something or someone is different or unfamiliar, ou may find yourself guarded rather than curious or open. By doing so, you miss chances to xpand your understanding of yourself, others and the world.

Vhen you show compassion and understanding to others, they are less likely to feel threat- ned by you, more likely to open up, and more willing to share their ideas. Co-operative olutions come from this safe place.

Humans tend to love certainty but often you don't know the answers and lack evidence sug- esting clear answers. There is always something you can do, even if you are in the darkest lace. It may be an internal shift or an external action. Acquiring wisdom is a life-long rocess which includes making your own mistakes and learning from them, becoming a keen bserver of life, and seeking wisdom from those you respect. Gradually, you learn to exercise our own discretion effectively and gain your own brand of wisdom.

Questions and Exercises

1. Can you think of times when you were guarded around people or situations, and doing so proved to be the right decision for you? Can you think of other times when the opposite held true for you? How did they compare?

2. When you've held leadership roles, or ones involving regular problem-solving, how have you handled those who held different views? How did you resolve differences? What did you learn about yourself? The others? Life?

3. Reflect upon and write down some of the most valuable pieces of wisdom you've acquired so far from your experiences, observations, mistakes, and/or from people you respect?

Notes

Notes

PART 2: SCHOOL/WORK

SECTION A: ROUTINES THAT ROCK

CHAPTER ELEVEN

SYNCHING HOME WITH SCHOOL, WORK, BUSINESS

The way you do one thing tends to be the way you do most things.
- Unknown

1. *Mindset Matters*

In the first part of this book, the focus was on love, courage and wisdom. The goal was to learn how to "live" these concepts through your thoughts, words and actions. The same logic and system is applied in this section. The seeds you plant in your mind about opportunities and challenges in school, at work or in your business, inevitably determine how you approach and respond to them. Eventually, you develop patterns of behavior characterizing your academic or working style. Therefore, what you initially feed your mind matters, because it obviously affects your planning and execution.

2. *Everyone is Different*

When it comes to certain things in life, routines can be exactly the life hack you need. Having systems for when, where and how to study or work, is invaluable. Each one of us has a different method based on our personality, our preferences, extracurricular and family schedule and workload. You may prefer working alone, in coffee shops or around family. Background music may or may not be playing. Your biorhythms also factor in. For example, you may be most focused right after you get home in the evening when ideas are still fresh, or you may need chill time and not settle down to do work until after dinner. Alternatively, you may be the most alert in the morning - even before having your coffee – and get your best work done before noon. The key is to figure out what works best for you.

For students, what seems universally helpful is having a regular place and time to complete your work. This includes a comfortable work space with proper lighting and air circulation. There's nothing like a stuffy room to de-motivate you and make you drowsy! Equip your space with commonly used supplies to avoid the frustration of having to look everywhere for a Post-It® note or stapler when you need it most.

3. *Adaptability - Don't Be a Slave to the Set-Up*

Change is inevitable, except from a vending machine.
- Unknown

Although routines are key, becoming a slave to them carries its own challenges. For instance, you risk becoming bored, humorless, or less motivated and creative. On the other extreme, you could find yourself becoming inflexible and unable to adapt to changes. Ironically, these changes sometimes include fun opportunities to play, socialize, or "unplug", which often re-energizes you and helps you do your work more effectively *and* in less time!

Again, the key is to find a system that works for *you*. Once you have a system, you'll find it easier to adapt it to fit your circumstances week to week and month to month. It's when you lack a system altogether that things can go sideways. Miscommunications with others becomes more common, and everyone's stress levels increase.

The next few chapters focus on the step-by-step process to realizing your goals, offering specific ideas to help you create routines that rock.

Chapter 11: Synching Home with School, Work, Business

Life Hacks

Mindset matters. The seeds you plant in your mind determine how you approach and respond to various challenges and opportunities at work or school. Eventually, you develop patterns of behavior characterizing your style. Therefore, what you initially feed your mind matters, because it affects your planning and execution.

Having systems for when, where and how to study or work, is invaluable. Everyone has a different method based on their personalities, preferences, extracurricular and family schedules, and workload. The key is to figure out what works best for you.

Don't be a slave to the set-up. Becoming a slave to routines opens you up to the risks of becoming bored, humorless, or less motivated or creative. On the other extreme, you risk becoming inflexible, irritable and unable to adapt to changes. Again, the key is to find a system that works for you, then adapt it to fit your circumstances over time. It's when you lack a system altogether that things can go sideways.

Questions and Exercises

1. What are some constructive thoughts you feed your mind about how to approach projects? What are some thoughts which don't seem to help you plan and execute effectively?

2. List the times, places, and techniques that function optimally for you when you're working on a school, work, or business project. Are there any clues or repeating patterns you can use to your benefit in different environments?

3. Name some ways you unplug, or take breaks, which usually re-energize you in ways that allow you to do your work more effectively.

Notes

Notes

CHAPTER TWELVE

THOUGHTS – DREAM, VISUALIZE, AFFIRM

Imagination is more important than knowledge.
- Albert Einstein

The intuitive mind is a sacred gift and the rational mind is a faithful servant. We have created a society that honors the servant and has forgotten the gift.
- Albert Einstein

1. Dream the Big Dreams

You've probably heard the expression "Dream Big" a thousand times. Dreaming engages your imagination. Here, you step outside yourself and live in the realm of possibilities versus limitations. Think of every great song, novel, comic book, movie, video game or piece of artwork you've enjoyed over the years. Or take a moment to contemplate the neat inventions that are part of everyday human existence. The ideas that lead to them were born in human minds, like yours!

There are tons of resources elaborating on this concept, some using scientific explanations, others using spiritual, philosophical or psychological perspectives. Most share one common thread, or life hack as I like to think of it...the power of your mind to impact your reality is astonishing.

The Monk Who Sold His Ferrari by Robin Sharma[28]* is one such resource. It's an inspirational tale about the path to personal development, effectiveness and fulfillment. In it, Sharma refers to "blueprinting", the two-fold process by which things are created. First, things must be created in the workshop of the mind. Secondly, they are created in reality[29]*. When you learn to manage your thoughts, dream freely, understand yourself, and expect a lot from your life, you set in motion a powerful process that can yield incredible results. And it all begins in your mind.

Allow yourself time to regularly imagine and dream. If you're having trouble, create a habit around it until it starts happening naturally. Consider the tips and example presented here and in the following chapters. Try out some of the ideas that resonate with you.

---

28 * Toronto: HarperCollins, 2007.
29 * 48.

Estrellita Gonzalez, author of *Face Your Acne: 10 Holistic Ways to Eliminate Acne*[30] is a big believer of dreaming and goal setting. She offers her own practice as an example for our readers:

I do my goal setting in January. I write down what I want to achieve that year, refer to it several times during the year, and then build ideas and plans around it. I do a series of things to help keep me on track:

- *Take my ideas and visualize them, especially the core idea I'm working on that year*
- *Express my gratitudes daily*
- *Review cards with various affirmations written on them daily*
- *Engage in positive visualization and self-talk daily, such as using "I AM..." statements I learned about through Wayne Dyer's work. That leaves little room for negative "I AM NOT..." beliefs and statements. Those are a sad waste of energy. They can lead to the very opposite of what I want, since I'll inevitably attract what I fear.*
- *Meditate regularly*
- *Adopt a mindset and action plan to consciously choose not to live around negativity*
- *Continue to dream, daydream and imagine possibilities!*

In addition to Estrellita's ideas, consider these tips to help you DREAM BIG:

- Talk about big ideas
- Spend time in nature
- Read books, blogs or articles that inspire you
- Spend time with amazing friends or mentors
- Watch less TV
- Write in your journal
- Remind yourself that anything is possible
- Breathe mindfully

There are scores of personality, aptitude and ability tests, also known as psychometric tools, which are specifically designed to give you individual feedback. They include The Birkman Method and Myer-Briggs Type Indicator (MBTI). You might find the test data useful to increase your self-awareness and self-management skills, as well as to guide your study, volunteer, career, or workplace goal setting. This can especially be useful when it uncovers information and options you hadn't even considered or known about before.

Classification systems can also have a dark side, though, so try to avoid pigeon-holing yourself (or others) or becoming overly dependent on the results. Also keep in mind that unlike IQ (Intelligence Quotient), which tends to stabilize in childhood, social emotional skills (EQ – Emotional Quotient) can be learned throughout life. Some personality traits emerge as you get older. Personality tests can even help identify areas you can target for growth, thereby expanding possibilities and dreams rather than limiting them.

Although the professional tests almost always charge a fee, students and employees may be able to access them for free or at a discount from their educational institution or workplace through the Career Services or Human Resources Departments. A free version I've found useful,

---

30 [*] She Power Publishing, Vancouver: 2016.

which combines the MBTI with a trait-based test, and is called the NERIS Type Explorer® can be found at www.16personalities.com.

An exercise which connects well with the upcoming section, is to look back at your life and list all the things you've done or experienced which have given you a measure of happiness and fulfillment. Now connect the dots, identifying common threads between them. Therein lie clues to some of your dreams and goals.

2. Visualize in Your Mind's Eye and Beyond

Vision boarding is a fun, easy and motivational tool. It can be done on a digital board or news-feed, such as social media apps, allowing you to collect, follow and/or post items. Items may include images, quotes and ideas that align with your personal vision. Or it might literally be a big magnetic or cork board you post things onto. Either way, you're creating inspiration from within yourself, using your own motivations and desires to guide you.

If you dream of being a scientist who helps the world address environmental damage, for in-stance, you might post images of prominent and inspiring environmentalists, logos of scientific organizations and educational institutions you want to be a part of one day, beautiful scenes of nature and animals and so on. You get the idea.

Your Vision Board not only becomes a daily concrete reminder of what matters to and truly motivates you, it helps you avoid distractions threatening to suck you away from pursuing your vision. It's also a marvelous life hack that counters the negative effect of endless media images that bombard your mind and sometimes make you question your vision in the first place!

3. Affirm as You Go Along

Inspirational Quotes

Never underestimate the power of a well-timed and eloquent quote! Even better is a collection of them at your instant disposal. Like vision boarding, a collection of inspirational quotes is a go-to life hack that focuses and motivates you to create your own fulfilling present and future.

Just like watching your TWA (thoughts, words, actions) and proper self-care, which we discussed earlier in this book, such quotes help you deal with stress and self-doubt. Use the techniques that work for you. Social media apps and the internet are useful friends. With them, you can find tons of motivating quotes from every source imaginable — books, movies, historical figures, poems, plays, spiritual guides.

In addition to the quotes attached to each of the chapters and topics covered in this book, I've included a sampling of some of my favorite motivational quotes.

Surround yourself with the dreamers and the doers, the believers and the thinkers, but most of all, surround yourself with those who see the greatness within you, even when you don't see it yourself.
- Edmund Lee

Your vibe attracts your tribe.
- Unknown

If you think you are too small to make a difference, try sleeping with a mosquito.
- Dalai Lama XIV

Appreciation is a wonderful thing; it makes what is excellent in others belong to us as well.
- Voltaire

Laugh when you can, apologize when you should and let go of what you can't change.
- Unknown

To succeed in life, you need three things: a backbone, a wishbone, and a funny bone.
- Reba McEntire

Be yourself; everyone else is taken.
- Oscar Wilde

What doesn't kill you makes you funnier.
- Unknown

Think big, act small, fail fast, learn rapidly.
- Unknown

Excuses that keep you safe...also keep you stuck.
- Alanis Morrisette

What you resist persists.
- Unknown

Don't be afraid to be open-minded. Your brain isn't going to fall out.
- Unknown

A bad attitude is like a flat tire. You can't go anywhere until you change it.
- Unknown

When life puts you in tough situations, don't say 'why me' say 'try me'.
- Unknown

Being challenged in life is inevitable, being defeated is optional.
- Roger Crawford

Please do not feed the fears.
- Unknown

Life is a dance between making it happen and letting it happen.
- Arianna Huffington

Your smile is your logo, your personality is your business card, and how you leave others feeling after an experience with you becomes your trademark.
- Unknown

It costs $0 to be a decent person.
- Unknown

Positive Mantras and Affirmations

Positive mantras and affirmations are short phrases that have the ability to calm, focus and empower you in challenging situations or during moments of self-doubt. Whether you say them in your head or out loud, they'll help move you in the direction you want to go *in that moment*. It's useful to have a few at your disposal, to repeat as necessary. Here are a few ideas to get you started:

1. *Go slowly.* This can be applied to anything you're doing. (Except driving in the left lane on the interstate and pulling off a bandage.)

2. *Om.* A sacred sound of Hinduism which means It is, Will Be, or To Become.

3. *I Am That I Am.* A famous line from the Hebrew holy book: Torah.

4. *All the love I need is within me now.*

5. *I can do this.*

6. *I am my own superhero.*

7. *Let [insert your name] be [insert your name].*

Chapter 12: Thoughts – Dream, Visualize, Affirm

Life Hacks

Dream the big dreams. Dreaming engages your imagination and allows you to live in the realm of possibilities versus limitations. The power of your mind to impact your reality is astonishing. Therefore, allow yourself time to regularly imagine and dream.

Visualize in your mind's eye and beyond. Vision Boarding, whether it's on a physical board or a digital one such as a social media app, is a fun and easy tool. It becomes a daily reminder of what matters to and truly motivates you, helps you avoid distractions and counters the negative effects of media images that bombard your mind and sometimes make you question your vision in the first place.

Affirm as you go along. Never underestimate the power of a well-timed and worded quote -or a positive mantra and affirmation - to focus, motivate and empower you, as well as to help you deal with stress and self-doubt.

Questions and Exercises

1. What are some dreams you've wanted to pursue but haven't yet acted upon or achieved? If you don't make time to "regularly dream", refer to Chapter 12 for ideas on how to create a habit around this. Which ones are you willing to try?

2. Look back at your life, and list all the things you've done or experienced which have given you a measure of happiness and fulfillment. Now connect the dots, identifying common threads between them. Therein lie clues to some of your dreams and goals.

3. Try vision boarding. Whether it's an actual board or a digital one, collect (or follow/ post) various images, quotes and ideas that align with your personal vision.

4. What are some of your favorite quotes? Refer to Chapter 12 or list ones you've found which inspire you. Add them to your Vision Board as well. If you don't already have a mantra or affirmation you regularly use, consider finding ones that resonate with you.

Notes

Notes

CHAPTER THIRTEEN

YOUR WORDS - PUTTING PEN TO PAPER

If you have a goal, write it down. If you do not write it down, you do not have a goal – you have a wish.

- Steve Maraboli

Vision without action is a daydream; action without vision is a nightmare.

- Japanese proverb

In the previous chapter, we discussed the importance of dreaming big and visualizing, as well as sustaining those pursuits using motivational quotes and positive mantras. In this chapter, we discuss the nitty gritty of planning.

To become reality, your ideas require action. Action includes making a *plan* for action. Regardless of what shape or size your dream is, by creating and exercising some control over a situation, you're being proactive. You're beginning with the end in mind, rather than leaving your situation to chance.

Don't worry. Your plans can always be revisited, revised and completely revamped if necesary. This could happen for various reasons: unanticipated opportunities, change of circumstances, new goals, shifts in your thinking and so on.

As the Japanese proverb above suggests, having a plan without acting on it keeps you in daydream mode. And yet, expending energy in the absence of a vision can result in mindless action. Both are fabulous recipes for disappointment or dissatisfaction, rather than personal success.

Angie Chik and Sim Sandhu understand the value of planning and acting. They co-authored the personal development book *Define and Defy: Unleashing Your Inner Potential*[31]. Both women had expressed the idea of wanting to write a book. They sought to inspire women and uplift those knocked down in life somehow, women who could benefit from motivation, perspective and powerful personal stories. They had a meeting of minds, attended a seminar together and the idea was born! Both became energized. It didn't stop there. They organized. They planned. Without the organizational and planning skills to write out the topics they wanted to address and clarifying the direction they wanted to go in, things would not have gone as smoothly as they did.

Angie and Sim cited many takeaways from this project, many of which mirrored my own when

---

31 [*] Markham: Authority Press, 2015.

I wrote this book. They include the following:

- The ability to discipline oneself is crucial. Many people want to write a book, but never get to it. They lack motivation. But mostly they lack the discipline.

- Clarity is king. Once they had clarity, they could deal with obstacles, because they already knew specifically what they wanted.

- Accountability and habits are success ingredients. Both authors wrote every day for over half a year and reported to one another. They found once they formed the habit, things seemed automatic.

As for planning your goals in the first place, Dr. Rupinder Toor acknowledges it's not easy to project far into the future nor is it always a good idea. In particular, if you're unclear, uninformed or considering various academic or career goals. If that's the case, she recommends a five-year timeframe. It's more "doable" and applicable to various stages of your life:

- Getting through high school
- Planning for post-secondary school and/or training
- Gathering information and advice, as well as volunteer or paid experience related to your areas of interest
- Undertaking future challenges (further education, work, volunteering, starting a business, specializing, etc.)

When asked what or who inspired her to become a doctor as well as start and run a non-for-profit women's health clinic, she recalls she was interested in sciences in high school and became fascinated by the human body. She wanted to learn more and so she pursued related studies. From the age of 18-23, she had a genuine interest in the health field and started on this path, not necessarily thinking about attending medical school. She researched various careers while completing a biochemistry degree, and decided medicine was the best fit for her.

At the time, there were no doctors in her social circle or family, although she was blessed with a passion for community service by her late father, and a strong spiritual base from her mother. Dr. Toor became a family doctor and practiced for several years before deciding to open a women's health clinic. She felt this shift afforded her the chance to make a unique impact and encompass all her experiences, talents and interests. She's been at it for over a decade now, gaining considerable experience and expertise, which she'd like share with other health care professionals across North America during the next phase of her career.

Dr. Toor couldn't have imagined she'd be doing this when she was 18, yet here she is and still as excited as ever. As she puts it, "when you live at the edge of your creative existence in life, it never becomes stale."

I hope the two examples presented have inspired you and got the wheels turning in your head. Next, I want to share specific suggestions for planning and goal setting, as well for anticipating and dealing with potential obstacles.

1. *Life Balance Wheel and Internal Motivation*

The secret of success is learning how to use pain and pleasure instead of having pain and pleasure use you. If you do that, you're in control of your life. If you don't, life controls you.
- Tony Robbins

The Life Balance Wheel is a fantastic life hack that allows you to self-assess and prioritize when it comes to goal setting.

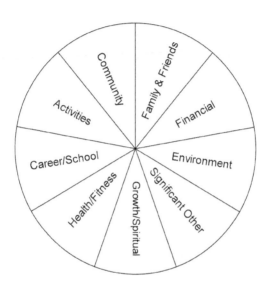

Have a look at the illustration and do the following:

- Identify the areas that apply to you and your stage (Young Adult, Adult, Parent, Divorced, Retired, etc.).

- Rank your level of satisfaction in each area (scale of 1-10 or 0-100%).

- Assess which area(s) you'd like to see improvement in. Know why you'd like to see the improvement. Is it just because everyone else is doing it? Or because it's relevant and a priority *to you*? Does it reflect your values in some way?[32] *

- Start forming goals in the area(s) you selected.

- Think about the areas you rated highly. What strengths and skills do you use here that could apply to the areas you'd like to work on?

---

32 * For a helpful exercise on identifying, grouping, and narrowing down your values, see https://www.cmu.edu/career/documents/my-career-path-activities/values-exercise.pdf

If you're feeling overwhelmed or have multiple goals for different categories, don't worry. Just pick the ones that seem the most immediate. Rome wasn't built in a day!

Finally, if you're unclear about whether a goal is appropriate or even reasonable, seek clarity. Who can you talk to who has knowledge or experience in this area? Or who can put you in touch with such a person? What resource(s) can you consult to get this information yourself?

As you start, keep in mind that major change is difficult for most people. Even minor changes to long standing patterns can be tricky. In both cases, having internal motivation and a game plan sets you up to succeed. Otherwise, the "drop out" rate is too high, no matter how well intentioned you are.

One way to kick start your motivation is this. For every area you'd like to see positive change in, think of the pain or displeasure associated with the current situation and associate the pleasure you'll feel when you achieve your goal. This allows you to hone in on your personal motivation - *your WHY* - and makes it easier for you to stick with your plan. A

2. *SMART Goal Setting*

What is SMART Goal Setting?

How often have you expressed a wish or a goal, only to forget about or get distracted with something else? You're not alone. Distractions are everywhere! However good your intentions, merely expressing a goal is a far cry from achieving it. Enter SMART goal setting, another little life hack worth familiarizing yourself with.

Effective and realistic goals - both short-term and long-term - are characterized by the following:

Specific
- Clearly articulate your goal. *I want to declutter and simplify my home (specific) vs. I want to declutter my life completely (general, not to mention overwhelming).*

Measurable
- Your goal must be easy to measure. *I want to clean out drawers/closets in all rooms (kitchen, bathrooms, bedrooms and garage) and sell/give away unused or unnecessary items.*

Attainable
- Set a realistic goal. *I'll work on project during my spare time in evenings and on weekends (2-3 days per week), devoting 2 weeks in total to each room, with extra time for the garage.*

Relevant
- Be clear about why and how this goal is relevant to you, and whether this goal achieves that. *By decluttering, I'll spend less time cleaning, organizing or looking for things, thereby freeing up time that I can spend with my kids or doing hobbies I enjoy.*

Time-limited
- Put a deadline on your goal. *I'll finish in 3 months (in time for a Spring Yard Sale)*

Be prepared to reassess and tweak your goals regularly. If you find you've taken on too much, you might sabotage your success. For example, there may not be enough hours in one season to declutter your home, join the Salsa Club, volunteer at the local Children's Hospital, and hold down your career and parenting responsibilities.

You'll want to determine the goals and commitments most important to you. Place your attention there first. Move onto the others once you feel you have things under control or know how much you can usually manage. It's better to do one or two things really well, than to do several things miserably.

If a goal is really big or longer term, such as organizing a school or work conference, split it into smaller manageable Action Steps. It might look something like this:

SMART Goal #1: Organize work team's 1st Technology Conference

Action Step #1: Choose date, book venue and equipment, advertise.

Action Step #2: Decide topics, invite speakers, finalize speakers.

Action Step #3: Do set up, including rooms, equipment, registration and name tags.

Breaking down goals helps you eliminate worry and overwhelm, and it pinpoints the steps can take immediately, or delegate! Moving forward this way supplies you with momentum needed to reach your ultimate goal.

Anticipating and Preparing for Obstacles

Insanity: doing the same thing over and over again and expecting different results.
- Einstein

Sound like something you've done in the past? Hoping this time when you start over, something will be different? We've all been there. To get a different result, you must do *something* different. One method is to know what roadblocks might be ahead and have potential strategies to overcome them.

GOAL: Organize Technology Conference	
OBSTACLE	STRATEGY
1. Co-ordinating volunteers to get conference organized in time.	1. Decide and set up meeting times in advance and communicate to volunteers early 2. Appoint committee leaders to brief anyone who has to miss a meeting 3. Assign specific duties to volunteers to avoid confusion and overlap.
2. Difficulty finding speakers.	1. Prepare list of topics for which we need speakers 2. Brainstorm with volunteers to come up with possibilities 3. Enlist help from managers, employees and personal networks

See the obstacle-strategy for the Technology Conference example. Do this exercise with one or more of your goals.

3. *Prioritizing*

Even if you've gone through all the steps outlined in this chapter, you may still find yourself with WAY too much to do and not know where to start. This is not an uncommon dilemma. How many times have we heard ourselves or others complain out loud, "I'm way too busy"?

In his book, *The 7 Habits of Highly Effective Teens*[33]*, Sean Covey talks in detail about "putting first things first." Prioritizing. The idea is that the better you organize yourself, the more you'll be able to do overall, including relaxing and just having fun! This gives you more control over your life, a sense of balance and higher performance.

There are specific methods and tips Covey offers to get organized and avoid counter-productive behavior. I've used tips from the teen guide but they easily apply to all age groups. I've recommended this system to many-a-client and used it myself for years until the system became automatic. As a planner by DNA, I consider it one of my favorite life hacks. I've summarized some of the key points of the Covey system here.

33 * Fireside: New York, 1998.

1. Procrastinate less. That'll produce less stress.

2. Learn how to say "no" to unimportant things that take you away from doing the important ones.

3. Cut down the time you spend on slacking activities such as TV, endless phone calls, time on social media, gaming, or any other time wasters you can think of.

4. Get a planner and start doing weekly planning:

    a. Note your key roles (student/employee, family member, volunteer, parent, friend, etc.).

    b. List the key things (2-3) you need to get done that week for each role.

    c. List the ways you will take care of your body, brain, heart and soul.

    d. Schedule your priorities and self-care activities into your planner. Over time, you'll notice whether you are over-scheduling. Symptoms include stress, exhaustion and not leaving yourself time to eat, drink, get place to place, and go to the bathroom!

    e. Things come up that require you to adapt your schedule, so don't be a slave to your planner! Gradually, you'll see patterns develop. Tweak things and build in some flexibility. It's an ongoing process, which helps you clarify the personal vision you have for yourself.

Chapter 13: Your Words - Putting Pen To Paper

Life Hacks

To become reality, your ideas require action. Action includes making a plan for action. Plans can always be revisited, revised and completely revamped if necessary. Having a plan without acting on it keeps you daydreaming. Similarly, expending energy without a plan can be mindless action.

When it comes to goal setting, the Life Balance Wheel allows you to self-assess and prioritize all the different areas of your life, and then move towards focused goal setting.

SMART goal setting is Specific, Measurable, Attainable, Relevant and Timed-limited. To help you stay on track, be prepared to reassess and tweak your goals regularly, to split bigger goals into smaller action steps, and to anticipate and prepare for obstacles.

Prioritizing. Staying organized and avoiding counter-productive behavior helps you do more overall, giving you more control over your life (including saying "no" to unimportant things), a sense of balance and higher performance. It also leaves you more time to relax and have fun!

Questions and Exercises

1. Rank your level of satisfaction in each area of the Life Balance Wheel in Chapter 13, assess which area(s) you'd like to improve, and start forming goals in the selected area(s). Consider the strengths and skills you selected in highly rated areas, and think of ways you can "transfer" these same skills to areas you'd like to work on. If you're feeling overwhelmed, or have multiple goals for different categories, don't worry. Just pick the ones that seem the most immediate.

2. Choose one or two goals you identified in Question 1, and make them into SMART goals. For each of the goals, list possible obstacles that might come up, and brainstorm strategies to deal with the obstacles.

3. What methods do you use to organize and prioritize? Are they effective, or could they use some tweaking...or revamping? Consult the Covey step-by-step method explained in Chapter 13 to help you with this.

Notes

Notes

CHAPTER FOURTEEN

YOUR ACTIONS - EXECUTION, CONSISTENCY AND PERSEVERANCE

Recipe for Success: Heat up an Idea, take Action, mix it up with Desire and Belief, then add a dash of Persistence.
- Unknown

There is nothing more powerful than an idea whose time has come.
- Victor Hugo (and Wayne Dyer)

First you dream, then you lace up your boots.
- Portia White, Canadian Opera Singer

1. *Execution – Practicing Effort with Ease*

I once heard the phrase "practice effort with ease" during a yoga class, and unlike the yoga move I was desperately attempting, the phrase instantly made sense to me. It suggested a way to have a great experience while doing something. It also pointed to a *gentler approach* to pursuing goals.

Let's discuss the first point. In his bestselling book *Flow: The Psychology of Optimal Experience*[34]*, Mihaly Csikszentmihalyi goes into detail about what makes an experience transcendent and genuinely satisfying: flow.

Flow is the state you reach when your conscious mind is no longer directing the show, when you're so "into" what you're doing that you lose yourself and things just happen with no conscious effort on your part. Athletes call it being "in the zone."

We've all been there. Flow is that state of being where you're so focused it's like time stands still. You don't have the attention to devote to irrelevant things or worry about your problems.

Csikszentmihalyi writes about all sorts of potential flow activities, from obvious ones like dancing, making music, playing games such as chess and so on, to less obvious ones like the joys of movement, seeing, tasting, writing and working.

---

34 * HarperCollins: New York, 1990.

When I heard the expression "practicing effort with ease," I was instantly reminded of the flow phenomenon. You can transform your goals to flow activities. Sometimes this'll be simple, because you're excited about something. Other times, you have to take steps to reach your ultimate goals, like mastering knowledge or learning skills you find boring. If, instead, you immerse yourself deeply into whatever task is at hand, practicing effort with ease so to speak, then your whole experience can be positively transformed. This applies to practice questions a professor assigns, cardio drills your dance instructor calls, or the guitar technique exercises your instructor recommends.

Now onto the second point. Practicing effort with ease is a gentler way of accomplishing your goals. "Effort with ease" almost sounds like an oxymoron, but it isn't. It means be intentional, work hard and stay focused, but also avoid becoming too attached to the results. You may do all the right things. You may read this book forwards and backwards, implement the suggestions and then boom, something happens you didn't expect or want. Or something you wanted and expected to happen doesn't happen. That's just life. Life is ever changing. Let me repeat that. *Life is ever changing.* For control freaks everywhere (present company included), this can be a game changing life hack.

Accepting that reality changes in ways that are often beyond our control and working with this fact rather than against it is a crucial success skill. To help you master it, I suggest you meet three of my friends, whom you may be familiar with: *Adaptability, Resiliency and Open-mindedness.*

Adaptability means you can adjust yourself readily to different conditions. Your boss gives your team an unexpected assignment. No problem. You possess the basic skills to complete it, have access to mentors as well as instructional online videos. You'll do the best you can. Besides, your co-workers are in the same boat as you.

Resilience refers to a person's capacity to recover quickly from tough situations. Tania's grandpa passed away a couple of weeks ago, and she was very close to him. She sticks with her plan to attend the Speaking Competition Semi-Finals. She's been preparing for months and decides to put in her best effort in honor of her grandpa's memory.

Open-mindedness refers to a willingness to consider new ideas or arguments. Sandeep feels his experience is limited when compared with many of his law school classmates. He is the son of hard working immigrants and the first one in his family to pursue a professional degree. Many of his classmates come from privileged backgrounds, and have travelled the globe before entering law school. One of his professors encourages him to join the student squash sports club and to apply for one of the student teaching assistant positions. Remaining on the fringes doesn't enrich his experience or earn him new friends, so Sandeep decides to go for it. Little does he know that the teaching assistant position he eventually accepts will inspire students from similar backgrounds to do the same in future years.

Adaptability, resilience and open-mindedness often develop when the game plan changes and people do *not* meet their goals or expectations. What are falsely labelled "failures" and "setbacks" are really just learning lessons. You come to know yourself better. You clarify your riorities. New and interesting pursuits arise. The process becomes easier and more enjoyable ver time. Effort with ease.

2. Consistency

don't fear the man who knows 10,000 kicks. I fear the man who has practiced the same kick 10,000 times.
Bruce Lee - Actor, Martial Artist, Philosopher

If you settle for progress, you will get something. If you aim for perfection, you will get nothing.
Unknown

What is the one and only thing you can do which will destroy your ability to achieve your goals? *Nothing.* In other words, *do* nothing. Raw talent and passion are excellent, but without effort and practice, you won't realize your goals.

The simple truth is that even small, consistent efforts eventually add up to produce huge results. Great habits are formed daily and require commitment. It might seem like a no-brainer life hack, but it can sometimes be hard to implement.

Think about it. If you've been going to bed far too late for as long as you can remember, it's going to take you some time to break this stubborn habit. By setting up new routines and making small steps every day, week and month, you'll end up with a healthier bedtime routine and won't be walking around like a zombie in the mornings. Consistency is key.

In his long work and life journey from his home country of Tobago in the West Indies to the U.K., and eventually to Canada, retired teacher and professor Brinsley Stewart learned important lessons. Brinsley taught at the junior elementary, high school and college levels. While it's easy to see another's success and assume it was easy, he notes, overnight success is not the norm. Focused effort and a strong work ethic *do* pay off. And, as he used to urge to his students and kids when they were young, the key is to "try, try and try again." He shares one of his favorite quotes about consistency, from poet and educator Henry Longfellow:

The heights by which great men reached and kept were not attained by sudden flight, but they, while their companions slept, were toiling upwards in the night.

3. Perseverance

It's a slow process, but quitting won't speed it up.
Unknown

If you are persistent, you will get it. If you are consistent, you will keep it.
Unknown

Most people fail, not because of lack of desire, but, because of lack of commitment.
Vince Lombardi

As the last quote above suggests, consistency and perseverance are related when it comes to achieving our goals. Perseverance is the determination shown in doing something *despite* difficulty or delay in achieving success.

In a great Forbes online article by Jason Selk[35], he talks about habit formation in the context of Tom Bartow's work. Bartow is a corporate trainer and business coach with Edward Jones. The things that might discourage or distract you from forming good habits or handling difficulties and delays may include the following:

- You struggle with positive habit completion and your old habits creep back up and threaten to take over again

- You allow negative results you experience to convince you what you're doing is not working and you are powerless to do anything about it

- You experience significant changes to your current pattern or schedule, such as holidays, illness, or even weekends

- You experience success and start to think you're special and don't have to do much to keep it up

Setbacks are normal and expected parts of life. Recognize them and roll with them. It's your willingness to do this, and not give up, that helps determine whether you'll reach a goal or not. That *is* the life hack here.

If that doesn't work, go back to your WHY. I'm talking about the pain associated with not achieving your goals and the pleasure associated with achieving them. If that still doesn't work, Bartow suggests projecting forward another 5 years and asking yourself what your life will be like if you don't start the changes now. Honesty with yourself is the best policy.

Consider the example of Dr. Toor, Founder and Director of Northeast Calgary Women's Clinic and recipient of a Queen Elizabeth II Diamond Jubilee award. Wayne Dyer's quote at the beginning of this chapter is one of her favorites: "There is nothing more powerful than an idea whose time has come."

Dr. Toor recalls her motivation behind creating her clinic and how she patiently worked her way through some of the obstacles that presented themselves:

When I started my career, I worked full time. And after I started a family, when my kids were little (0-5), I felt they needed me the most, so I put my full-time career on hold. Once they were in school, I focused on my career again and thought about what I really wanted to do with it. With the women's clinic I founded and run, I realized it was the best fit of my skills, talents, cultural and life experiences, and language skills. It allowed me to make a unique impact. In a regular family medicine practice, I didn't feel like that and thought there were others who could do the job just as well as I could. Uniqueness is important.

---

35 * April 15, 2003.

As for choosing to work as a non-for-profit, I really wanted to serve my community and not have it be solely a money-making venture. Although I wanted to get paid reasonably for the work I did, it wasn't my #1 motivator. But I truly believe that the money will come when you are doing "that thing" you were meant to do. And that's exactly what happened. In fact, I made more than what I expected.

I took one step at a time when it came to establishing my clinic. I had no business experience. But I figured out what I needed to do to get the appropriate licenses, approvals and clinic space. Then I needed to buy exam beds, so I researched and figured that out. I did it as I went along. Whatever needed to get done, got done. I experienced financial barriers, unanticipated start-up costs and so on. I just dealt with them when I had to. And I started getting cheques in the mail from various organizations, some of them for large amounts. And I was able to use these to start the clinic.

As for remaining focused, I focused on the idea. It became urgent, and "no" wasn't a possibility for me. What I've received from it is very fulfilling work – a night and day difference from what I did before. I didn't feel like I was making a real difference before. Now it feels like a calling. Personally, it's about way more than financial reward. Professionally, I'm surprised at how well I'm recognized and underestimated how it really does positively impact the whole community. Finally, it's also opened many other doors, some completely unforeseen, such as teaching, policy planning, and community outreach.

Chapter 14: Your Actions - Execution, Consistency And Perseverance

Life Hacks

One way to have a great experience while doing something is to practice effort with ease, or flow. Flow is a state of experience where you are so focused it's like time stands still. It also applies accomplishing your goals. It means be intentional, work hard and stay focused, but also avoid becoming too attached to the results. Life is ever changing, after all. Three friends to help you with this process are adaptability, resiliency and open-mindedness.

Raw talent and passion are excellent, but without effort and practice, you'll face unrealized goals. The simple truth is that even small, consistent efforts eventually add up to huge results.

Perseverance is the determination shown in doing something despite difficulty or delay in achieving success. Challenges and setbacks are normal and expected parts of life. Recognize them and push through them. It's your willingness to do this, and not give up, that helps determine whether you'll reach a goal or not.

Questions and Exercises

1. Think of experiences you've had where you literally lost track of time while engaged in them. How did you feel? Imagine doing that with more and more activities in your life. Challenge yourself to do this when engaged in activities you have to do, but which are not your favorite things to do.

2. When the unexpected happens, how do you typically react? Think of a particular situation you'd love a second attempt at. Knowing what you know now, how could you have made more (or different) efforts to adjust? What could you have told yourself in order to help you move into action more effectively? Whose help could you have enlisted?

3. Pinpoint a time when you stuck with something important, and made consistent efforts that paid off somehow. What kept you going? What positive habits did you form? How could you apply these habits to other areas of your life? Conversely, think of a time when you broke a bad habit. How did you do it? What did that tell you about yourself?

4. If you found yourself attached to the outcome, how could being open to the outcome have helped you?

5. Have you ever given up too early? You are so close to your goal, but for some reason you gave up? What prompted you to give up? What would have happened if you stuck with it? Think of a time when you did stick with it despite difficulties and delays. How did that feel?

Notes

Notes

SECTION B: SEIZE OPPORTUNITIES

CHAPTER FIFTEEN

STRENGTHS AND CHALLENGES

The pursuit of excellence is gratifying and healthy. The pursuit of perfection is frustrating, neurotic, and a terrible waste of time.
– Edwin Bliss

Your playing small does not serve the world.
– Marianne Williamson

1. *Cultivate Key Strengths*

Jonathan Michael, who counsels people using The Birkman Method, shared an amusing story about cultivating your key strengths. As a young man, Jonathan was gifted and interested in many disciplines: literature, philosophy, math, music, languages, strength training. You name it, he had an aptitude and hunger for it. One day, one of his mentors was frank with him and explained the 22 Slices of Toast analogy:

You have one spoonful of jam and what you're trying to do is take it and spread it on 22 pieces of toast. There'll be so little jam on each piece that you'll fail to enjoy any of them. Why don't you lather that jam on 2 pieces of toast and enjoy every last morsel instead?

The life hack here is straightforward. Of the pursuits you excel and are interested in, choose a few and focus your energies there. By trying to become an expert in all of them, you run several risks:

- Spreads your time and energy really thin
- Diminishes your enjoyment of one or all of them
- Prevents you from being really good at any one thing
- Increases your stress behaviors, such as impatience, anger, anxiety, fear
- Leaves you feeling disappointed, inadequate and unhappy if you're not careful

Just because you *can* do more, doesn't always mean it's a good idea. By taking on less, you often achieve more. How? Well to start, you'll decrease or eliminate many of the risks listed. Now you're poised to achieve and truly value mastery and excellence in your life. This is not about perfectionism. It's about creating the conditions under which you can do your best.

If Jonathan's advice makes sense to you but you find yourself grappling with perfectionism, consider the 3 Ps. I first heard of them from my friend Anna St. Onge, author of *Convent Girl: Life Growing up in Canadian Convents*[36] The 3 Ps are *Perfectionism*, *Procrastination* and *Paralysis*.

To demonstrate how the 3Ps can sabotage you, consider the scenario below or substitute with one that applies to your life. I lived through a major renovation so this one's close to my heart. The home renovation your family's undertaking leaves the house, including the office where you normally do your work, a royal mess. This happens the week you have to finish your Theatre & Film project. You have no space to work on your poster board, much less find the supplies you need to put it together.

Perfectionism: You're always used to working in a very tidy space and convinced you need this to start your project and do the perfect job.

Procrastination: You put off starting your project, because you're not sure how to proceed or you're afraid you won't do a good job. You wonder if the teacher will grant you an extension.

Paralysis: You're unable to take action towards your project. You feel so overwhelmed with stuff all over the place, how much there is to do, and you don't know where to start...so you don't.

Don't worry, you're not the only one who's been in this boat. Anna's twist on the 3 Ps is the 4th P: *Puttering*. The antidote to paralysis is to put one foot in front of the other and just *move*. One little step at a time, until you can take bigger steps for longer. Clear everything off the office desk, pile the items in a corner and place your poster board on the desk. Next, look for a few supplies you'll need right away: scissors, glue and markers. If you can't find them, buy the essentials or borrow them. Then, just get going. Or if that's not possible, consider asking your friend if you can do your project at her place. Eventually, you have a finished project to hand in, no extension required.

2. *Make Challenges Your Friends*

Bad times have a scientific value. These are occasions a good learner would not miss.
- Ralph Waldo Emerson

You need to learn how to select your thoughts just the same way you select your clothes every day.
Elizabeth Gilbert - *Eat, Pray, Love*

Challenges find you, whether you're looking for them or not. You can't predict what'll happen from moment to moment, even if you have a vision, plan and practice good habits like consistency and perseverance. All of that makes it much more likely you'll get what you're seeking, but not always.

For example, we all have weaknesses. Add to that the fact we may lack the skill, knowledge, or interest in mastering something. However, what's missing may be a pre-requisite to obtaining something you really do want. You have the motivation. What matters is how you're going to approach challenges and weaknesses in your life. I'm talking about your *mindset*.

36 * CreateSpace: USA, 2016.

Earlier in the book, you read about how an attitude of gratitude shapes your thoughts, words and actions. Later, you saw how adaptability, resiliency and open-mindedness help you approach your goals in a healthy way so you can *practice effort with ease.* All of these things help you face challenges.

Here, I want to explore mindset choices further. Firstly, you *have* choices, as the Elizabeth Gilbert quote suggests.

Secondly, become aware of *what* your choices are. They're divided into empowering and self-defeating thoughts at the end of this section. These come from Steve Mensing, a self-help and emotional growth author and retired counsellor. He's created an excellent website called Self-Helpapedia dedicated to sharing techniques that optimize your emotions, beliefs and behaviours.[37*]

As you review the lists below, ask yourself which thoughts you identify with more often, what influences you to choose one over the other, whether you're satisfied with your choice, and which mindset inherently sounds more appealing.

Thirdly, make the decision to consciously *shift* to more empowering mindsets. Make challenges your friends. Learning from challenges also helps ease the pain of losses you experience. Some shifts will happen quickly, just with your increased awareness. Others will be like bad habits. It'll take time to break them and build good ones.

Self-Defeating Thoughts

- I shouldn't make mistakes, lose or fail. If I do, I'm no good. (Perfect Performance)
- It's impossible to overcome my life challenges or solve my problems. I can't be happy. (Impossibility)
- Others will not accept, love or care about me if I make mistakes or if I'm flawed.
- I must impress others and/or have their approval or I will be rejected, go unnoticed, and be unworthy. (Approval anxiety)
- If I believe something strongly enough, it'll happen without me taking any action.
- My value as a person goes up or down by my achievements, beauty, intellect, status or possessions; otherwise I'm worthless. (Failure phobia)
- There must be something wrong with me, so why bother? (Inferior/defective)
- I believe something without the evidence to support it.
- I should always be happy, in control and confident. (Emotionally Perfect)
- I took all the right steps and worked very hard, yet didn't get rewarded and praised, so I feel cheated.
- Others should change or do as I demand, so that I can be happy and not frustrated. (Behavior expectation)
- I must not disagree, argue, or raise conflicts with people important to me. (Conflict Fear)
- I should please others, even if it makes me feel bad or my life goals are put on hold.
- Life should be easy, and I should never be frustrated or denied. (Frustration Intolerance)

---

37 * http://www.self-helpapedia.com.

Empowering Thoughts

- I speak compassionately to myself, "What would I say to a close friend in this situation?" (Double Standard Method)
- I look for the evidence for and against my belief or claim about myself. (Examine the Evidence)
- Rather than just thinking about something, I experiment and take on the challenge to see what happens in real life. (Experiment Method)
- I ask friends, teachers, parents and others how they would feel and think if they were in a similar situation to me. (Survey Approach)
- Instead of blaming or putting myself down, I examine the situation and figure out what factors contributed to this difficulty and what can be done to solve it. (Reattribution Method)
- I rephrase what I say about myself, my challenges and my weaknesses in more positive ways and leave out negative, insulting and emotionally charged labels. (Relabeling Approach)
- I create a double column and note down the benefits or costs of believing something. (Pro & Con Technique)
- I use specific words like *sometimes or infrequently*, rather than using unconditional and judgmental words like *never, always, total failure, forever*. (Specify Rather Than Globalize)
- I evaluate an activity based on the effort I put in, what I learned of value, or the satisfaction and pleasure I took from doing it, rather than just on the outcome. (Outcome Versus Process)
- I look for the humor in the situation or in my own silly thoughts and worries about a situation. (Humor)
- Instead of an "all or nothing" black and white approach to something, I see the average, gray, or middle grounds. (Thinking in Terms of Gray, Middle Grounds)
- I look at something as a fact of life and accept it as (delete: something that) "it happened." (Fact of Life Acceptance)
- I focus on my behavior and traits, rather than focusing on myself. Failing the science test does not make me a total failure.

Be patient. Practice. Expect setbacks. Try again. Perfection is not the goal. The incentive to reframe thoughts and move from wallowing in self-defeating to feeling empowered is SIGNIFICANT. It's a life hack you will use over and over. It'll improve satisfaction in ALL aspects of your life: your relationships, academics, career, extracurricular activities and overall physical and emotional health.

3. When to "go for it" and when to "let it go"

Given that we all have weaknesses and challenges, a logical question to ask is, "When should you go for it and when should you just let it go?" After all, you don't have the time, energy and desire to take on every single challenge you face on a daily basis or every weakness you identify. If you did, there's a good chance you'd lack life balance and be stressed out all the time.

Remember, you've got a lot of the fundamentals under your belt already. In Part I, you learned how it all starts at home with mindsets, behaviors and routines that set you up for personal success. These same strategies help you enjoy and succeed in your school, work, career and personal life. Building on those fundamentals, you learned the theory and practice of visualizing, planning well, prioritizing and following through with consistency and perseverance.

Through this process, you've likely acquired a good deal of self-awareness, self-management and relationship skills. This gives you the ability to assess any given challenge and weakness that comes your way, and determine how to think about it and handle it. Over time, with more knowledge, skill and experience, you'll refine your vision and goals. As a result, you may approach the same challenge or weakness in a different way. For example, your values or priorities may have shifted due to increased knowledge or experience. Often there is no one right answer or way of doing things. This, of course, brings us to our next topic, the perils of comparing yourself to others and how to overcome them.

Chapter 15: Strengths and Challenges

Life Hacks

Cultivate Key Strengths. Of the pursuits you excel and are interested in, choose a few and focus your energies there. By taking on less, you often achieve more. Now you are poised to achieve and truly value mastery and excellence in your life.

Make Challenges Your Friends. Choose productive mindsets to deal with inevitable challenges. Become aware of empowering and self-defeating thoughts you have. Make a decision to consciously shift to more empowering mindsets, and put in the effort to make that happen. Be patient, practice, expect setbacks. Perfection is not the goal. This approach will propel you forward in ALL aspects of your life.

When to "go for it" and when to "let it go". Through the process outlined in the book, you've acquired a remarkable amount of self-awareness, self-management and relationship skills. This gives you the ability to assess any given challenge and weakness that comes your way, and determine how to think about it and handle it. You may approach the same challenge or weakness in a different way in the future. There is not always one right answer or one way of doing things.

Questions and Exercises

1. Identify your strengths, and the pursuits you excel and are interested in. Which ones really grab you?

2. If you find yourself struggling with perfectionism in one or more areas, consider whether you fall prey to the 3Ps (Perfectionism, Procrastination, Paralysis). Apply the antidote (Puttering) and think of small steps you can take to move forward, however small. Then just keep going till those steps get bigger!

3. Review the list self-defeating and empowering thoughts in Chapter 15. Consider which self-defeating thoughts you run into the most often. Which empowering thoughts can you consciously shift into in order to deal with challenges more effectively.

4. Which challenges or weaknesses seem the most important to you right now? How do they relate to your priorities and values?

Notes

Notes

CHAPTER SIXTEEN

COMPARISON - FRIEND OR FOE?

Comparison is the thief of joy.
- Unknown

The reason we struggle with insecurity is because we compare our behind-the-scenes with everyone else's highlight reel.
- Steve Furtick

1. *Distinguishing Inspiration, Comparison and Unhealthy Comparison*

Humans have a tendency to make upward comparisons. Being inspired by others can be very motivating, whether it's family members, friends, classmates, historical figures or anybody who seems to be a master in their arena. There are so many talented, curious and committed people in this world, past and present. They'll be amazing role models to you throughout your life.

Such upward comparisons are not bad in and of themselves. They definitely give you standards for what's possible, likely, or effective. They also give you all sorts of valuable information you use in everyday life. Think about the last time you looked at consumer reviews for a product, restaurant or service. What if you have to evaluate human resources software systems in order to choose one for your growing business? Comparisons allow you to examine things in detail and reflect on them, noting similarities and differences.

However, the dangers of comparing *yourself* to others are revealed when you use the results of your examination to pass constant, inaccurate, negative, or unnecessary judgments about yourself or others. This is not only counterproductive, but can be unhealthy and *painful*.

It's like comparing your inside to someone else's outside. Social media apps make it easy to do. Click and scroll, and you easily find yourself scrutinizing the way you look, what you own, where you vacation and how you spend your time. You're often unaware of a person's unique set of circumstances, yet you may easily compare your skills, talents and accomplishments to theirs. Not exactly objective scientific date, is it? For example, you may have limited or no information of their:

- Previous skills, knowledge, training and/or experience
- Practical, emotional, financial supports and resources
- Expectations and pressures from family members, community or culture
- Personal values, passion or focus
- Available time to dedicate to something

2. *Pitfalls of Constant, Inaccurate and/or Unhealthy Comparisons*

Years ago, when my daughter was in the second grade, we had a memorable conversation on the way to school. She enthusiastically described her classmate's fabulous new home where she'd been a few days before. *"How great would it be to have a huge house like that Mom?"* And then, with a touch of sadness and disappointment in her voice, she said, *"He's so lucky."*

I agreed with her that her friend's house sounded big, beautiful and fun. Being the coach that I am, I also talked about the difference between inspiration and comparison and how the first is almost always good, the second not always.

As time goes on, I pointed out to her, she'll always notice someone she thinks who is smarter, more athletic, more musical, more artistic, has more, etc. And there's always going to be someone with a bigger house, fancier devices, more luxurious car, more stylish clothes, etc. It's a never-ending cycle with a never-ending number of people and situations to compare yourself to.

I felt like I had gone on long enough (or too much) and asked her whether I made sense to her. She said she thought so and asked whether it was kind of like that Rolling Stones song lyric that goes, *"You can't always get what you want, but if you try sometimes, you get what you need."* Given her passion for singing, my daughter sang the line. I was blown away, not only by the fact that she remembered the song, but that she applied it to what we were talking about. She had figured out the life hack! I just wish I had nailed that one by Grade 2!

The pitfalls of engaging in constant, inaccurate and/or unhealthy kinds of comparisons are many. Try to avoid them as best as you can! They include the following:

- Promotes self-defeating behavior that robs you of the enjoyment of living. You move away from your own vision and become hyper-focused on doing more, being more and having more. All in an effort to keep up with others, or in the belief that it'll lead to success and happiness.

- Supports self-deflating thoughts. You feel like you don't "measure up" to others' abilities and accomplishments.

- Demotivates you, preventing you from pursuing your goals or trying new things. You convince yourself others are so much further ahead, so what's the point of trying?

- Encourages a scarcity mentality, instead of an abundance mentality. This is the belief that there is "not enough pie to go around" and, therefore, it's best to be selfish rather than generous.

All these pitfalls are more relevant now than ever before with the widespread use of social media, where people routinely post selective moments and accomplishments. Viewers often consciously or unconsciously compare their entire lives to these brief snapshots. The result? Negative thoughts and feelings about themselves.

Doesn't sound fun, does it? Well, there's a much better alternative. Compare yourself to you, not others. See the next section for ideas.

3. Focus on Your Own Growth

Earlier, you saw the drawbacks of comparing yourself to others when you don't really know or appreciate their unique set of circumstances. You lack deep knowledge and understanding about their true values, focus, life experience, strengths, victories, challenges, fears, pressures, health, etc.

On the other hand, you're the leading expert on *you*. You have firsthand knowledge of your circumstances. Your expertise continually grows as you become more self-aware, which in turn allows you to manage yourself more effectively.

When you compare yourself to who *you* were last year, last month, last week, or even yesterday, your results are naturally more objective and accurate. Despite the fact your moods may fluctuate and you might be kinder to yourself on some days rather than others, you're still comparing yourself to your former self. Not someone else. This is a valuable life hack. It saves you so much energy in needless comparison with others.

And if you've been following the system for SMART goal setting (Specific, Measurable, Attainable, Rewarded, Time-limited) outlined earlier, you have another tool in your toolbox to track your own vision, not someone else's. Basically, you're comparing and competing against who you're capable of being.

Academically, and with extra-curricular activities, if you've worked hard on establishing regular habits - study and practice - over time you'll notice improved results and performance. From here, you can decide whether to continue along the same track or tweak things further.

During conversations, and especially during conflicts, you'll know if you're using kinder words more often (e.g. "I" vs. "You" statements) or listening more deeply and asking more questions before drawing conclusions. This may translate to less conflict, increased patience and a general sense of well-being.

With your physical health, you'll know you're making smarter food and activity choices when you have more energy, better sleep and more stable or elevated moods.

All this feedback you receive from yourself about yourself pays dividends. It's a positive way to move forward in your life, stay true to yourself and not fall prey to constant distractions. Say goodbye to the endless and vicious cycle of comparing yourself to others and say hello to Empowerment 202.

Chapter 16: Comparison - Friend or Foe?

Life Hacks

Distinguish inspiration, comparison and unhealthy comparison. Comparisons are not bad, in and of themselves. However, the dangers of comparing yourself to others are revealed when you use the results of your examination to pass constant, inaccurate, negative and/or unnecessary judgments about yourself or others.

Pitfalls of constant, inaccurate and/or unhealthy comparisons include demotivation, promoting self-defeating behavior, supporting self-deflating thoughts that you don't measure up and encouraging a scarcity mentality instead of an abundance mentality.

Focus on your own growth. You're the leading expert on you. You have firsthand knowledge of your circumstances. When you compare yourself to who you were last year, last month, last week, or even yesterday, you're comparing and competing against who you're capable of being.

Questions and Exercises

1. Who have you compared yourself with, in the past or present? How has this inspired you, or given you standards for what is possible or likely? When and how has it given you valuable information?

2. Now think about when it has led you to compare yourself unfairly to someone else? What do you *not* know about them or their circumstances? What are some of the pitfalls you've personally experienced as a result of comparing yourself this way?

3. How can you compare yourself to you in relation to who you were last year, last month, last week, or even yesterday? How are those results more objective and accurate?

Notes

Notes

CHAPTER SEVENTEEN

GIVE BACK

We are driven by self-interest; it is necessary to survive. But we need wise self-interest that is generous and co-operative, taking others' interests into account. Co-operation comes from friendship, friendship comes from trust, trust comes from kind-heartedness. Once you have a genuine sense of concern for others, there's no room for cheating, bullying or exploitation.
- Dalai Lama XIV

Be the change you want to see in the world.
- Mohandas Gandhi

Life's most persistent and urgent question is, "What are you doing for others?"
- Martin Luther King Jr.

1. *All for One, and One for All*

The motto "All for one, and one for all" originally appears in the nineteenth century novel by French author, Alexander Dumas, *The Three Musketeers*. It means that all members of a group must support its individual members and the individual's commit to supporting the group.

This motto, along with the Dalai Lama quote, support the same view: we're all in it together. When we understand and accept our shared humanity, our empathy increases. We realize that by helping others – those near and dear to us as well as those who aren't directly connected to us - we're actually helping ourselves. This is not only a valuable life hack, it's a deep one.

The list of real and potential benefits that come with your commitment to this kind of thinking is long:

- Provides you with deep emotional satisfaction.
- Gives you spiritual well-being and a life with deeper meaning.
- Boosts your health. Your happy hormones increase when you help others. Your stress hormones decrease when you know you're supported.
- Grants you increased knowledge and understanding as you connect with different people and situations around the world.
- Affords you the chance to express gratitude for all you have by sharing it with others.
- Offers you natural leadership and mentorship opportunities. As you lead by example, you're really "walking your talk."

- Gives you problem-solving practice and ways to express creativity.
- Presents you with occasions to share your time, energy and expertise for important causes.
- Provides you with chances to learn more about yourself and what interests you, which helps you define your purpose and vision in this life.

2. *No Act of Kindness is Too Small*

If you think you are too small to make a difference, try sleeping with a mosquito.
- Dalai Lama XIV

In the previous chapter, we discussed some of the pitfalls of unfairly comparing yourself to others, including the rise of self-defeating and de-motivating thoughts.

Self-defeating thoughts make you feel like you don't "measure up" to others' abilities and accomplishments. Demotivating thoughts persuade you others are so much further ahead so there's no point trying.

The same logic applies to giving back. If you start comparing yourself to others' efforts, rather than viewing them as inspiration and motivation, you risk not doing anything at all. If everybody thought this way, the planet loses out big time.

The powerful thing about kindness is you can practice it in every moment, of every day, of every year. It's a habit and a mindset. Once adopted, you naturally look for ways to give back, big and small. And opportunities appear out of nowhere. Over a lifetime, small acts of kindness add up to *a lot* of good. Here's a list of "small acts" you've no doubt benefited from or done for someone else:

- Opening a door for someone
- Giving up your seat on the bus
- Smiling and making eye contact with the salesperson helping you
- Giving a genuine compliment
- Helping a friend understand a difficult math concept
- Welcoming a new person into a group activity
- Donating all your loose change in a year to the local food bank
- Contributing used coats and blankets to a collection drive
- Shoveling snow for a sick or elderly neighbor

Karima Bawa recalls one of the most important lessons her late mother taught her:

Charity and philanthropy don't just mean writing big cheques and getting recognition for doing so, but are often small acts that make a huge impact in someone's life. These can be done on a daily basis, and often just involves sharing the person you are with someone who can benefit from that.

Angie Chik shares a personal story of "giving back." Angie is medical science researcher, piano teacher and co-author of *Define and Defy: Unleashing Your Inner Potential.*[38*]

---

38 * Authority Press: Markham, 2016.

started playing the piano at age 7 and never looked back. My parents took my sister and me to a music store and asked us which instrument we wanted to learn. I gravitated towards the piano. However, it wasn't until I met my seventh piano teacher (out of 10) during my 10 years of formal piano education, that my life changed. My eyes opened. This teacher was creative in a way I hadn't ever experienced before.

The result is that I'm still playing the piano, learning new pieces at my own pace, and experiencing the rewards of sharing music with others, young and old. When I was in high school and volunteering at a seniors' home, I saw a piano in the corner of the dining room one day and started playing it for fun. Some keys were missing and it was badly out of tune, but once I finished Chopin's piece "Fantasie-Impromptu," I looked up to see almost a room full of seniors sitting in a semi-circle behind her, some with watery eyes. Others personally thanked me. That's the moment I realized the true power I had to affect people through my playing. Not only that, piano playing has afforded me a beautiful escape and way of attaining peace of mind.

I love to tune in on social media to Angie's piano playing and that of her tabla-playing (tradiional Indian drum) co-author Sim Sandhu. It's moving and mesmerizing!

3. Antenna for Assisting

The world is changed by your action, not by your opinion.
— Paulo Coelho

If you feel compelled to compare how you're doing when it comes to giving back, use your previous self as the guidepost. What you'll quickly notice is that it's like flexing a muscle. The more you flex, the stronger you become, the heavier the weight you can handle.

Before you know it, you may even be setting SMART goals around giving back that align with your vision. Hebah Hussaina, a student at University of British Columbia in the Faculty of Science and a TEDx speaker, is passionate about helping others. In her TEDx talk called "How Volunteering Grows Healthy Communities," she shares her story of falling in love with volunteerism at the ripe age of twelve, when she helped out at an art camp for little kids. She was inspired by a little child in the art camp who lacked the finger dexterity to properly hold a crayon or paintbrush.

A few years later, at the age of fifteen, Hebah started a non-for-profit called Youth for CARE, which inspires youth to contribute to the local hospital and community. One of their programs is 3D Printing. They have partnered with organizations to provide 3D print assistive technology to children with neurodevelopmental conditions, so they can participate in everyday activities like wielding a paintbrush to create their own artwork. Not surprisingly, Hebah focused her Integrated Sciences degree in this area of study. Hers is an inspiring story of vision and the power of giving back.

Chapter 17: Give Back

Life Hacks

All for one, and one for all. When we understand and accept our shared humanity, our empathy increases. We realize that by helping others — those near and dear to us as well as those who aren't directly connected to us - we're actually helping ourselves. This can give us deep emotional satisfaction, health boosts, spiritual well-being, increased knowledge and so forth.

No act of kindness is too small. If you start negatively comparing yourself to others' efforts, rather than viewing them as inspiration and motivation, you risk not doing anything at all. The powerful thing about kindness is that you can practice it in every moment, of every day, of every year. It's a habit and a mindset. Over the course of a lifetime, small acts of kindness add up to a lot of good.

Giving back is like flexing a muscle. The more you do it, the stronger you become, the more you can handle.

Questions and Exercises

1. Think of the times and ways in which you've helped others in a meaningful way. What have you gained from these experiences? Make an exhaustive list.

2. Pinpoint times when you could have made a small but perhaps not noticeable difference. Now multiply this instance by several points every day, of every week, of every year. How could that have made a cumulative difference in the lives of others?

3. What are some natural skills or talents that you could share with others, to make a difference? What are some organizations, events, or occasions at which you could share them?

Notes

Notes

PART 3: PLAY

CHAPTER EIGHTEEN

CULTIVATE YOUR CREATIVITY

Time you enjoy wasting isn't wasted time.
- John Lennon

Only boring people get bored.
- Unknown

1. *What is Creativity?*

Growing up, I loved school and sports. I still do. My parents, especially my dad, encouraged and actively supported me. As I experienced success, my motivation and interest only grew. Arts and music were never emphasized in my parents' household, nor in the families they were from. Aside from listening to music recreationally, I didn't pay much attention to the arts. In fact, I convinced myself I wasn't even artistic, musical, or even creative!

My closest friend throughout grade and high school, Sheryl, was a gifted artist. Her sketches and artwork were amazing, and she even designed my graduation dress for me. I thought she was the creative artist and I was the athletic nerd. To top it off, my one attempt at being musical failed miserably. I tried out for the part of Dorothy in the school play of Wizard of Oz. The music teacher cut my audition short after the first two lines of the song *Somewhere Over the Rainbow* and told me *I needed more work.* I became convinced I shouldn't be torturing anyone with my voice and even stopped singing the national anthem during school assemblies. I just mouthed the words. The good news was I got a part as a dancing neon poppy. It was pretty sophisticated choreography for a grade school play. So at least I thought I had dancing potential. I laugh at the whole thing now.

I share this story for a few reasons.

Firstly, I had limited exposure to the arts growing up, resulting in a limited understanding and appreciation for it. This changed over the years as my social circle and experiences grew more diverse. I developed a more open-minded and curious attitude, not to mention I just had a lot of fun with music and the arts.

Secondly, I falsely evaluated my abilities based on an embarrassing but impactful sixth grade audition, as well as an unrealistic comparison to my talented artistic friend. As I matured, I realized the limitations I was placing on myself with some of the stories I was telling myself *about* myself. I now wish I could go back in time to share some advice with my music teacher about giving kids constructive feedback!

Thirdly, I thought of creativity as narrowly applying to arts and music, rather than what it actually is: *the ability to transcend traditional ideas, rules, patterns, relationships and to create meaningful new ideas, forms, methods, interpretations, etc.*[39]*

Dr. Brené Brown, author of *Gifts of Imperfection*, is spot on in her description of creativity:

"I'm not very creative" doesn't work. There's no such thing as creative people and non-creative people. There are only people who use their creativity and people who don't. Unused creativity doesn't just disappear. It lives with us until it's expressed, neglected to death, or suffocated by resentment and fear.[40]*

2. Why Prioritize Creativity?

This is where we get to the "what's in it for me?" life hacks about creativity.

Opens the Door to Opportunities

Why is creativity an important life skill? Dr. Shimi Kang, in her bestselling parenting book, *The Dolphin Way* (Penguin Books: Toronto, 2014), writes about this in detail. In addition to critical thinking, communication and collaboration, creativity is identified as a core skill needed to "do well in today's fast paced, highly social, ultra-competitive and globally connected world..." (84). In other words, cultivating it will open doors to all sorts of opportunities for you down the road. Or put more bluntly, the inability to think and act creatively limits your options and potential.

Everyday Success Skill

When you think about how you relate to others, consider all the creative problem solving you've done over the years with friends, family members, classmates and co-workers.

How good does it feel to resolve a conflict in an unexpected way that doesn't leave one side feeling victorious and the other side feeling like garbage? Or how gratifying is it to solve a group project problem in a totally surprising way, or to come up with a novel sports play that catches the opposing team off guard? These are all examples of creativity at work.

The peace and co-operation that comes from generating creative solutions just gives you further incentives to engage this way.

All the attitudes and skills discussed throughout this book are aimed at giving you the confidence and security for this exact moment: to express your creativity without fear. This is how effective leaders are shaped. You have all the knowledge and tools to accomplish that.

---

39 * Dictionary.com.

40 * Hazelden Publishing: Minnesota, 2010 (96).

You get to be YOU

"Play" is another arena you may assume is creative by definition. But not all play is created equal or equally creative. Confused? Let's take an example. On a trip to India with her family many years ago, my good friend Lucki Kang was visiting her family's village. She observed a couple of kids using her older son's empty juice boxes and straws to fashion a dollhouse, little stick figures and miniature furniture. She was amazed. The kids' parents were very poor, but that didn't hold these kids back from exercising their creativity to make their own entertaining make-believe world. Today's toy store dollhouses often arrive ready made from the factory with a uniform look, layout and wardrobe. Minimum assembly required. Unfortunately, minimum creativity required too.

So not only is it fun to be creative, it's personally meaningful to express your originality. This applies equally in your home, school, work, volunteer, extracurricular and leisure life. And it's not something that can and should be compared to what others do, because it's something uniquely *you*.

Larry Beryar, the former competitive hockey goalie and now official guitar student and enthusiast, offers this insightful John Lennon quote: *"Time you enjoy wasting isn't wasted time."* This speaks to pursuing what you love. Others may criticize you, but if it's something you truly enjoy and get value from, it is not wasted time. When he was growing up, a lot of people told Lennon he'd never make a living playing guitar! They told him he was wasting his time. Just shows you, you have to be true to yourself.

3. *How to Cultivate Your Creativity?*

Now comes the easy part.

The first part of this book emphasized how learning to love and respect yourself enables you to love and respect others more fully. That includes the way you think, talk and act towards yourself and others. The link to creativity is this. When you take care of yourself, your creativity flourishes. Dr. Kang explains it this way:

Creativity and critical thinking require a balanced state of mind. Lack of free time, stress and external pressure are all well-known creativity killers. In contrast, sleep, play and social partnership are powerful enhancers of creativity and critical thinking. (264)

Besides taking care of yourself and engaging with others, the best way to cultivate your creativity is to *go create*! I like this particular life hack, because it feels like a green light to just go out and play, for my own good!

You may have plenty of ideas on how to do this. Included here is a list of various pursuits that will tap into the creative genius that already resides within you.

- Write a short story, play or poem; do a parody of an existing one
- Sketch, doodle or paint something
- Design, knit or sew something
- Make an entertaining scrapbook of your last family vacation
- Compose a piece of music or lyrics to a song
- Cook something new or do a seasonal twist on a favorite dish
- Decorate your room with things you find interesting
- Choreograph and do a dance routine to a favorite song
- Take snap shots of anything you find interesting
- Build something from existing materials you find at home
- Take a course or workshop, or watch a You Tube video or Ted Talk on anything creative you'd like to know more about.

You get the idea. The next chapter delves further into how you discover these interests.

Chapter 18: Cultivate Your Creativity

Life Hacks

Creativity is the ability to transcend traditional ideas, rules, patterns, relationships...and to create meaningful new ideas, forms, methods and interpretations. We all have it.

Cultivating creativity is fun, opens doors to future opportunities, allows you to solve problems and conflicts in unexpected ways, and enables you to express your originality in personally meaningful ways.

When you take care of yourself, creativity flourishes. It also flourishes when you just go out and create! Write a story, design something, cook something new, decorate your room, take pictures, take a course or watch a video on something new you'd like to learn.

Questions and Exercises

1. Recall times when you and/or others were able to solve problems or conflicts in unexpected ways. What did you observe, about yourself and others?

2. What are some personally meaningful ways in which you express your creativity? How often do you make time to do this?

3. If you find yourself lacking time or opportunities to express your creativity, think of ways you can carve out time and space to do so. Who could help you? What kinds of things interest you?

Notes

Notes

CHAPTER NINETEEN

CURIOUS ADVENTURER

Anyone can memorize facts and figures.
The real way to learn anything is to go out and experience it and let your curiosity lead you.
- The Man with the Yellow Hat, from Curious George the Movie

1. *Identifying a Curious Adventurer*

You may have heard the expression, "curiosity killed the cat". It's an idiom usually used to warn people to mind their own business and not pry into the affairs of other people. That's not the curiosity we're going after here. We're aiming more for the Curious George variety.

Curious George books have been around for ages. They feature the adventures of a curious monkey named George. As the quote at the outset implies, curiosity is a key to learning. When you're curious, you're interested and eager to learn something.

2. *Does curiosity really matter?*

Curiosity is a key to self-motivation. In *The Dolphin Way*, Dr. Kang talks about how humans and animals, such as dolphins, are driven by their natural curiosity and desire for knowledge. When you're in balance, your curiosity fuels your motivation for learning and keeps it going.[41]* It's an amazing cycle...and a life hack that just keeps giving.

As if that's not enough, Dr. Kang also points out that curiosity calms you down too. You're way less apt to judge or react to something when you view it with curiosity. Instead, you observe and interact.

As a curious adventurer, you will benefit throughout your life. For example, you'll discover new and hidden talents. You'll continually learn about yourself, others and the world, making you a more interesting person. Rather than focusing on what's probable, you'll open your mind to what's possible. You naturally come to appreciate life as a gift, not something to be taken for granted. And best of all, the life of a curious adventurer is *way* more fun. You'll never be guilty of being that "boring person who gets bored."

Estrellita Gonzalez spoke about her curiosity this way:

Curiosity drives a lot of the things I've done. Living an adventurous life is part of my philosophy. Behind it is the idea that I make my reality.

---

41 * Penguin Books: Toronto, 2014 (236).

I was shy as a kid; that is, until my dad threw me into his restaurant business as a server. I then opened up quite a bit and after graduating high school, I suggested to my friend that we go backpacking in Europe. I didn't approach these kinds of experiences with trepidation; rather, I viewed them as opportunities to explore. A fearlessness developed within me, prompting me to start my first business at the age of 25. Even when I worked for others, I never lost sight of my desire to run my own business. My need to be creative drove this. When I think about it, I realize both of my parents had worked in various industries throughout their lives. My dad was a welder in his country of origin, then became a hairdresser when he immigrated to Canada. Later on, he ran his own restaurant, and then finally, he moved to South America and ran a fishing business.

Not surprisingly, I exposed my son Enriqué to many pursuits, so he could discover for himself what he had a knack or passion for. He has always been an improviser, his own man, and never shy of performing or speaking in front of large groups. Eventually, he was exposed to acting through a classmate of his, and it totally resonated with him. Neither myself or his dad had been involved with acting, though his dad and maternal grandma had been involved actively in the creative arts. Enriqué had found a gift, and has been actively acknowledged by the professionals he has worked with, and now has developed quite a passion for it. Curiosity leads to all sorts of wonderful things!

3. *Channeling Your Curious Adventurer*

Now that you know the "what" and "why" of being a curious adventurer down pat, let's get to the how-to. Mindset is critical. The good news is that you've done most of the work to develop the right mindset. Throughout this book, I've emphasized key principles that remove barriers to curiosity or actively help you foster it. Essentially, the life hack here is to get out of your own way! Here's a re-cap:

- Be open, kind and gracious with your thoughts, words and actions (towards yourself and others)
- Practice love, courage and wisdom every day
- Take care of yourself (body, mind, soul) and you'll feel balanced
- Learn and practice good communication techniques
- Try new things
- Play in nature
- Ask a lot of questions
- Don't give up

All these things foster your natural curiosity and sense of adventure.

Chapter 19: Curious Adventurer

Life Hacks

Curiosity is a key to learning. When you're curious, you're interested, inquisitive and eager to learn or know something.

Curiosity fuels your self-motivation for learning. You are way less apt to judge or react to something when you view it with curiosity, and more apt to observe and interact.

Channel your curious adventurer...try to be open, kind and gracious with your thoughts, words and actions; practice love, courage and wisdom every day; take care of yourself; learn and practice good communication techniques; try new things; ask a lot of questions; and don't give up.

Questions and Answers

1. Think of specific times when your curiosity has led you to new learning and possibilities, whether at home, work, or school, or while you're travelling or out in the community.

2. Identify potential barriers to curiosity that you might be experiencing. Consult the "Channelling Your Curious Adventurer" section of Chapter 19 for a list. What areas could you chip away at?

3. Another technique to cultivating curiosity is to seek out "curiosity" role models - people you know who seem interesting and inquisitive. What qualities or habits have you observed in them?

Notes

Notes

CHAPTER TWENTY

DRIVE CAREFULLY

With your head full of brains, and your shoes full of feet, you're too smart to go down any not-so-good street.
- Dr. Seuss

The future lies before you, like a field of snow;
Be careful how you tread it, for every step will show.
- Unknown

The title of this chapter and the quotes illustrate a guiding principle in this chapter. Use your smarts to avoid making destructive decisions. You'll come across many opportunities and risks throughout your life. How you handle them matters.

In the last chapter, we promoted seeking adventure as essential to living a full life that includes fun, learning and meaning. Throughout this book, we also talked about how mistakes are amazing learning opportunities. All that is true. However, there are some false steps that can permanently alter the course of your life. If managed improperly, they can limit your opportunities, seriously damage your growth and even have devastating consequences.

This may seem contradictory to the themes presented elsewhere in this book, but it's not. Risk taking itself is not bad, especially when you're aware of the possible or probable outcomes. These include uncovering hidden talents and passions, helping others and exposure to new growth and opportunities. When you're aware, you make better decisions. When you're not, bad things can happen. It's that simple. It's a life hack you don't want to leave home without.

Although fear of consequences can be a strong motivator, that's not the intent here either. Knowledge is power. Becoming aware of this knowledge gives you the power to manage three common risks you and those you care about may encounter.

Though this discussion is aimed more at our younger readers, it can very easily be adapted to other readers and issues. For example, drunk driving is an all-ages problem. Similarly, academic dishonesty has parallels in the workforce, community organizations and interpersonal relationships. Within all of these, you will find people lying, cheating or falsely taking credit in order to gain various advantages.

1. *Reckless and Drunk Driving*

It's not a coincidence that teens and young adults have more legal driving restrictions and higher car insurance rates than adults. They simply lack the years of experience adults have, both in driving as well as in managing the freedom and responsibility that comes with that privilege.

While fearlessness can be a noble trait when taking on new challenges and learning, if it's unchecked it encourages an "I'm invincible" or "Nothing can happen to me" attitude. This can promote unsafe, reckless, and/or drunk driving. This leads to far too many car accidents that end in death and injury. Add to that the negative outcomes that accompany this loss: criminal and civil penalties; legal and medical issues; emotional and psychological feelings of grief, regret and guilt.

Unfortunately, none of this is exaggerated. MADD (Mothers Against Drunk Driving), a prominent organization in this area, reports the sobering facts and statistics on their website[42]*:

- *Young people have the highest rates of traffic death and injury per capita among all age groups and the highest death rate per kilometer driven among all drivers under 75 years of age. More 19-year-olds die or are seriously injured than any other age group.*

- *Motor vehicle crashes are the leading cause of death among 16 to 25 year olds, and alcohol and/or drugs are a factor in 55% of those crashes.*

- *16-25 year olds constituted 13.6% of the population in 2010, but made up almost 33.4% of the impairment-related traffic deaths.*

Though the goal is to dramatically decrease injuries and fatalities due to reckless and drunk driving, the sobering reality is that there are still far too many preventable tragedies.

Personal responsibility (i.e. personal power) can never be underestimated. MADD offers comprehensive information, statistics and strategies to prevent drunk driving, among them the following:

- Exercise basic driving caution, such putting on your seatbelts, following the rules of the road and so forth
- Resist the pressure of your peers to engage in underage drinking and worse, to drink and drive, or agree to be passenger in a car with a driver under the influence
- Contact a parent or trusted family member if you need a ride

Whether it's removing yourself from a potential drunk driving situation, drug use or another uncomfortable scenario, consider making an agreement with your parents to have an escape route. Blogger and parent Bert Fulk devised an easy and discreet hack to do it: The X Plan[43]*.

---

42 * www.madd.ca.

43 * February 23, 2017 https://bertfulks.com/2017/02/23/x-plan-giving-your-kids-a-way-out-xplan/.

You text the letter "X" to one of your parents if you find yourself in a sticky situation, and a few minutes later your parent calls or texts back. You exchange a simple script in which your parent informs you that something's come up, you'll be picked up in a few minutes and you'll be told more once the parent picks you up. Presto! Danger, social ridicule and discomfort successfully avoided.

2. *Teenage Pregnancy*

Having and taking care of a baby, as well as parenting a growing child, is a life altering experience and amazing privilege. It's also all-encompassing and physically exhausting. The typical teen lacks the skills, knowledge and resources needed to handle a pregnancy and motherhood. Even if she possesses the necessary maturity, patience and ability to handle stress, there's no escaping the reality that her current and future educational opportunities, career choices and partner options will be more limited or altered than her non-pregnant peers.[44]*

Dr. Rupinder Toor approaches teen pregnancy prevention as a poverty issue:

If we want thriving individuals, families, communities and countries, where does that all start? Who is the core of that? It's often women, as they tend to invest in others, as opposed to just investing in themselves. So focus on the women. How do you do that? Educate them. Why don't we do that? Early marriage in many developing parts of the world, and teen pregnancy in North America and other developed countries, cut off opportunity and set up a vicious cycle. One generation misses out, and often, so does the next. So, educate the girls.

Dr. Toor lights up when she describes the magic of youth:

Youth is such an incredible time of physical energy and hope, discovery of self and the world, obtaining education and experience. It is the foundation for shaping and pursuing your lifelong dreams, which may or may not include having kids down the road. As a teen parent, a big chunk of this youth will be spent caring and paying for the needs of a child, not on exploring your own potential and wider contribution to the world.

If, after considering all the obstacles and future effects on her life and career, a teen is still convinced that she's ok with teen motherhood, she also has to know that she's likely making the same choice for her child. If she thought about it, would she truly believe that it's in the best interests of her child? What parent doesn't want to give their child the best opportunities to reach *their* full potential, be happy and contribute to the world? These opportunities require parents who have maturity, knowledge and, you guessed it, financial resources. Computers, hockey equipment, vacations, college – they all cost money!

Finally, the very fact of getting pregnant in the first place, even if it doesn't result in the mother keeping the baby, can have huge and lasting impact. The stress, hormones and health risks associated with teen pregnancy, as well as the physical, emotional and psychological effects of ending a pregnancy, are heavy matters. Not surprisingly, many parents, schools and community leaders invest time and care to educate youth about teen pregnancy and parenthood.

---

44 * "Effects of Teenage Pregnancy" by Julia Bodeeb, last updated April 14, 2015, LIVESTRONG.com http://www.livestrong.com.

3. *Academic Dishonesty*

Bad behavior is a really BIG topic that can cover everything from foul manners to committing serious criminal offenses. It's beyond the scope of this book to cover all these important issues in detail, including crime, effects of drug use, as well as online and personal bullying. These topics are discussed very openly in today's society and you're encouraged to do so, whether it's in your home, school, place of worship, or during your other activities. There are also credible online and print resources you can consult.

I'm going to touch on one piece of bad behavior: academic dishonesty. Given the highly competitive nature of the university admissions process, academics, as well as job and career markets, this topic is especially relevant.

Academic dishonesty covers an array of things, most commonly the following:

- Cheating - giving or obtaining assistance without due acknowledgement during a formal academic exercise, such as an exam

- Plagiarism - using or copying the ideas, words or statements of others without proper acknowledgement

- Fabrication – falsifying data, information or citation

- Sabotage – doing something to prevent others from completing their work (e.g., disrupting work or cutting pages out of library books)

- Deception – lying to a teacher regarding a formal academic exercise (e.g. giving a false excuse for missing a deadline, lying about having submitted work).[45*]

Consequences of such misbehavior may include lowered marks, school suspensions or expulsions, as well as permanently altered academic records. These things can limit your future opportunities to qualify for scholarships, gain entry to university or other post-secondary programs, or be accepted for certain jobs, careers and internships. This is serious business.

There are also intangible losses of academic dishonesty. Things like your values, ethics, integrity and character. These define who you are and how you conduct yourself on a daily basis, which includes your academic life.

When you cheat, you may pay a big external price. If you get away with it, you may be tempted to do it again. This sets you up for repeating and escalating risks in school, at work, in your personal lives. Either way, you'll pay a big internal price, too. Lost ethics. Lowered integrity. Tainted character. Diminished confidence in your own abilities. None of them sound like your best self. If you do get caught, you'll likely lose the trust and respect of those *you* respect, including loved ones. People are not born cheaters. They become cheaters.

45 * Source: Berkeley City College website (http://www.berkeleycitycollege.edu/wp/de/for-students/what-is-academic-dishonesty/).

Chapter 20: Drive Carefully

Life Hacks

Unsafe, reckless, and/or drunk driving leads to far too many car accidents that end in death and injury, especially among teens and young adults. Add to that the negative outcomes that accompany this loss: criminal and civil penalties; legal and medical issues; emotional and psychological feelings of grief, regret and guilt.

Teenage pregnancy. The typical teen lacks the skills, knowledge and resources needed to handle a pregnancy and motherhood. The very fact of getting pregnant in the first place, even if it doesn't result in the mother keeping the baby, can have huge and lasting impact.

Consequences of academic dishonesty may include lowered marks, school suspensions or expulsions, as well as permanently altered academic records. These things can limit your future opportunities. There are also intangible losses, like your lowered integrity, tainted character and diminished confidence in your own abilities. People are not born cheaters, they become cheaters.

Questions and Exercises

1. Have discussions with your friends, parents and loved ones on the topic of unsafe, reckless and/or drunk driving. Have a strategy in place for what to do or say in case you find yourself in potentially dangerous situations.

2. Pregnancy, sexuality, gender issues, and harassment are important yet sensitive issues. Who can you consult with on these issues who is knowledgeable, safe and reliable? What resources are available to you in the community, at school, at work, in your home, on the internet?

3. There have been high profile cases in the media of academic dishonesty and falsified university admission applications. Admissions processes and built-in institutional and societal privilege have also come under fire. Reform is slow. What are some strategies you can choose individually to ensure you don't fall prey to academic (or life) dishonesty? What are some group actions you can take or support which may help?

Notes

Notes

CONCLUSION

The aim of this book is to serve as a thoughtful and practical life hack guide on your ever evolving happiness journey, and to living your best life. That doesn't mean you have to be perfect. That is NOT the goal. None of us is perfect.[46] Rather, the goal is to practice love, courage and wisdom in every area of your life. And to reap the benefits of doing so.

An analogy that Dr. Toor shared with me is that of a computer's operating system. When a computer is virus-free, up-to-date and handled with care, the computer usually runs smoothly. It does what you need it to do. When it glitches, slows down, or just doesn't start up, you need to pay attention. It might need maintenance, updates, or entirely new programs!

Similarly, you get feedback about your *own* operating system. What is the current quality of your relationships, body, mind and heart? Feeling content? Energetic? Motivated? Uninspired? Frustrated? Too much conflict? Repeated negative patterns? All of these states give you valuable feedback to think and act upon. It might be telling you that you're on the right track, and to just keep doing more of the same. Fabulous!

Or it might be giving you clues about which areas need some more attention. That's a call to action! You're not alone. The ready-to-use life hacks in each chapter are here to help you. Practically and theoretically. After all, the stronger your WHY for each life hack you try, the more likely you'll follow through.

Practice more love, courage and wisdom in your daily thoughts, words and actions.

Question your ideas and be open to other ways of thinking and being.

Take care of your body.

Create effective routines.

Implement some of ideas you've been thinking about.

Incorporate dreaming and visualizing, goal setting and action plans.

Find ways to give back, have fun and adventure, and find creative pursuits!

Eliminate unhealthy comparisons.

Find inspiration, joy and meaning.

Be compassionate with yourself, and others.

And most of all, define your own path. YOLO!

---

46 * Or if you look at it through a spiritual lens, all of us have perfect souls.

CPSIA information can be obtained
at www.ICGtesting.com
Printed in the USA
LVHW080316261019
635429LV00006B/108/P